Praise for *Usable Usability*

D0117964

"A new look at the fundamental principles behind what makes stuff usable from Wise Reiss. And practical advice about how to go about it. This one is going onto my bookshelf."

—SUSAN M. WEINSCHENK, PH.D., author of *100 Things Every Designer Needs To Know About People* and *Neuro Web Design*

"After reading this, you'll wonder how so many products with flawed usability ever get to market, and be determined that nothing you are involved in makes the same mistakes again. Eric Reiss successfully distills an entire career's worth of making things easier to use into a book packed full of practical tips and examples for novice designer and experienced practitioner alike."

—MARTIN BELAM, Lead User Experience & Information Architect, Guardian News & Media

"Practical, easy to read, packed with a lifetime of experience, Usable Usability *is guaranteed to make your product or web site easier to use."*

—GERRY McGOVERN, author, *Killer Web Content* and *The Stranger's Long Neck*

"The understanding of usability should not be confined to the design community—it has immense philosophical importance. Far too many things in modern life are conceived by and for the System Two brain, forgetting the fact that it is less-talkative System One brain which makes most of the decisions—and which generates the greater part of the pleasure and irritation produced by our experiences. Eric's book is a tremendous addition to this vital debate.

—RORY SUTHERLAND, Vice Chairman, Ogilvy & Mather UK, author *The Wiki Man*

"A refreshing and pragmatic perspective on a central topic—definitely worthwhile."

—HARRY MAX, Vice President, Experience Design, Rackspace

"Ask Eric Reiss for advice about making something more usable and you're likely to hear about anesthetized turtles, bad airline service, and vacuum cleaner bags. Every page is an opportunity to experience Eric's wit and wisdom, but it's all in the service of a wonderfully practical guide to usability."

—DAN WILLIS, Associate Creative Director, Sapient (can also be found at www.uxcrank.com)

"If you're serious about creating great user experiences, this is a must-read book! Eric's insights on usability are reinforced with delightful examples and are presented with a business-smart perspective that few others can match."

—Richard Dalton, Senior Manager, Experience Strategy & Measurement, The Vanguard Group

"Today, good usability isn't just 'nice to have'—it's a business imperative! In this brilliantly useful, exceptionally usable book, Eric Reiss explains exactly what you need to do to improve your products, your services—and your bottom line. Read it before your competitors do!"

—Michael Seifert, CEO, Sitecore Corporation

"With Usable Usability Eric Reiss has authored a new classic; seasoned UX practitioners, fledgling designers, and anyone interested in creating memorable experiences will find it insightful, engaging and inspirational. Make a place for it on your bookshelf/eReader!"

—Matthew Fetchko, digital strategist

"The issue of usability is no longer a concern only to a few specialists, but is now a required area of awareness for anyone participating in product or service design. This book is brimming with ideas for how to make things not only usable but also seductive."

—Atsushi Hasegawa, Ph.D., President and Information Architect, Concent, Inc.

"As the author says 'In the simplest terms, if a product works, you'll use it'. And Eric's book works. I was amazed at the plethora of familiar situations that he has described which we all face daily, the issues we grapple with in frustration, the precious time we lose, all because a product was released without proper usability testing. The carefully selected illustrations and examples in the book certainly pass the usability test, and along with Eric's fine sense of humour, I guarantee a fun read."

—Kiran Mehra-Kerpelman, Director, United Nations Information Centre

"What a great book! Eric Reiss has put together astute observations he has gathered over the years (and from around the world) on usability. Guidelines for reducing uncertainty and making users feel intelligent round out this excellent volume. These make a comprehensive manual for anyone in charge of decisions on how to make things—including everything from utensils to interfaces—more simple, more unobtrusive, and just more usable. Did I mention it's a great book?"

—Jay Rutherford, Professor of Visual Communications, Bauhaus University

Usable Usability

ERIC REISS

Usable Usability

Simple Steps for Making Stuff Better

WILEY

John Wiley & Sons, Inc.

Usable Usabilty

Simple Steps for Making Stuff Better

Published by
John Wiley & Sons, Inc.
10475 Crosspoint Boulevard
Indianapolis, IN 46256
www.wiley.com

Copyright © 2012 by John Wiley & Sons, Inc., Indianapolis, Indiana

Published simultaneously in Canada

ISBN: 978-1-118-18547-6

ISBN: 978-1-118-22755-8 (ebk)

ISBN: 978-1-118-24043-4 (ebk)

ISBN: 978-1-118-26519-2 (ebk)

Manufactured in the United States of America

10 9 8 7 6 5 4 3 2 1

For general information on our other products and services please contact our Customer Care Department within the United States at (877) 762-2974, outside the United States at (317) 572-3993 or fax (317) 572-4002.

Wiley publishes in a variety of print and electronic formats and by print-on-demand. Some material included with standard print versions of this book may not be included in e-books or in print-on-demand. If this book refers to media such as a CD or DVD that is not included in the version you purchased, you may download this material at http://booksupport.wiley.com. For more information about Wiley products, visit www.wiley.com.

Library of Congress Control Number: 2012939589

To my parents,
Louise and Eric Reiss,
who showed me how the efforts of
a few passionate individuals
could change the world.

CREDITS

ACQUISITIONS EDITOR
Mary James

PROJECT EDITOR
Maureen Spears

TECHNICAL EDITOR
Lynn Boyden

SENIOR PRODUCTION EDITOR
Debra Banninger

PRODUCTION EDITOR
Katie Wisor

COPY EDITOR
Charlotte Kughen

EDITORIAL MANAGER
Mary Beth Wakefield

FREELANCER EDITORIAL
MANAGER
Rosemarie Graham

ASSOCIATE DIRECTOR OF
MARKETING
David Mayhew

MARKETING MANAGER
Ashley Zurcher

BUSINESS MANAGER
Amy Knies

PRODUCTION MANAGER
Tim Tate

VICE PRESIDENT AND EXECUTIVE
GROUP PUBLISHER
Richard Swadley

VICE PRESIDENT AND
EXECUTIVE PUBLISHER
Neil Edde

ASSOCIATE PUBLISHER
Jim Minatel

PROJECT COORDINATOR, COVER
Katie Crocker

COMPOSITOR
Maureen Forys, Happenstance Type-O-Rama

PROOFREADER
Nancy Carrasco

INDEXER
Robert Swanson

COVER DESIGNER
Ryan Sneed

ABOUT THE AUTHOR

Eric Reiss has been meddling with service- and product-design projects for longer than he cares to remember. Today, he is CEO of The FatDUX Group, an international user-experience design company headquartered in Copenhagen, Denmark. Eric has also lectured on design principles at the Bauhaus University in Weimar, is a former Professor of Usability and Design at the IE Business School in Madrid, and serves on the advisory boards of several universities and institutes in both Europe and the United States. His *Web Dogma*, a design philosophy that transcends both fashion and technology, has been adopted by 1000s of developers and companies around the world. You can follow Eric Reiss on Twitter: @elreiss.

ACKNOWLEDGMENTS

A lot of people were involved in the creation of this book. These include the thousands of anonymous artists, writers, educators, politicians, soldiers, and clerics who have shaped my views on usability. And then there are the many design professionals I've met who triggered some thought process I can no longer track back to its source. Thank you. I remember your ideas if not always your names.

That said, there are four individuals who have been particularly influential: Claus Møller, who introduced me to Scandinavian Service Management back in the 1980s; Ray Considine, who showed me how service and conversion went hand-in-hand; Philip Crosby, the Total Quality Management guru, who demonstrated why "zero defects" should be everyone's goal; and Mogens Sørensen, my mentor for many years in the advertising business, who showed me how form and function could be united to create truly wondrous things.

All my FatDUX colleagues around the globe have been incredibly supportive throughout the project. Here in Denmark, Maiken Kjærulff spent many days optimizing photos, adjusting text templates, and commenting on my initial rough drafts. Many thanks to one and all!

My longtime friend and voice of reason, Lynn Boyden, provided superb editorial assistance and technical editing. I followed most of her suggestions; if you see stuff you don't like, I take full blame. And Lynn will undoubtedly say "I told you so."

I'm grateful to Marcel Douwe Dekker, Matthew Fetchko, Mark Hurst, Kishorekumar62, Peter J. Meyers, Anders Schrøder, SEOmoz, John Smithson, and the Wikipedia Project for providing photos, screenshots, and other images.

The entire Wiley team has been brilliant. Mary James, my patient acquisitions editor, shepherded the book from concept to contract, working closely with my good friend and legal representative David M. Saltiel. Maureen Speers, my project editor, smoothed out the rough passages and really got the show on the road. Charlotte Kughen, my copy editor, kept the prose flowing and spelling correct. And Deb Banninger, senior production editor, and Katie Wisor, production editor, actually turned everything into a real book! I am so very, very grateful.

And finally, a big hug and kiss to my wife, Dorthe, for putting up with all this nonsense. And yes, I promise to stop taking so many pictures of doorknobs and salt shakers—someday.

—Eric L. Reiss
Copenhagen, Denmark
June, 2012

CONTENTS

INTRODUCTION

The word "usability" drives me nuts. "User friendly" is even worse; it's one of those expressions, like "awesome," that has become so overused as to lose all meaning. Search for *usability* on www.amazon.com and you'll get more than 4,000 hits—almost twice as many hits as for "web design." Maybe this is why inexperienced web designers often fall back on usability "statistics" to defend their work instead of making it better.

Of course, despite the constant overuse of the term and misuse of the research, a lot of us in the industry have long known that "usability" is indeed the secret to business success, online *and* offline. So, I'd like to share some thoughts, observations, and facts with ordinary people who are simply out to produce better stuff using common sense rather than politics to get things done.

I'll start by defining the key concept.

What is "usability"?

So you can put this book in proper perspective, here's my definition of usability:

> Usability *deals with an individual's ability to accomplish specific tasks or achieve broader goals while "using" whatever it is you are investigating, improving, or designing—including services that don't even involve a "thing" like a doorknob or web page.*

Pretty simple, huh? Here's how it works:

If a car won't start, its basic, functional usability is bad. If the car starts but is unsafe, unreliable, or merely uncomfortable, the car still has usability issues, albeit slightly more indirect. But here's the point: In all of these instances the usability of the car relates to our situational needs. That means our *satisfaction* with the experience affects the quality of the usability, too. If we are going on a long, relaxed road trip, comfort is important. If it is raining and our neighbor offers us a ride to work, convenience takes precedence over comfort. And even if the vehicle doesn't run at all, it can still provide shelter, become a place to play, or serve as an object of study (think homeless people, children climbing on old fire-engines in playgrounds, and car museums).

Online, we may be talking about load times, navigation, graphic layout, the size of buttons. It's all about usability.

If you accept this basic definition, you see that usability isn't restricted to website design, mobile apps, ATMs, and other onscreen experiences. Personally, I see usability issues all around me—from the way my can opener works in the kitchen to how my passport works in a distant country[1]. As a collective term, (and for lack of a more high-falutin' technical phrase) I call all of this stuff "stuff." The upshot is that usability in my vision goes beyond the pedantic "links should be blue" advice you often hear. That's also why you see more than just the standard screenshots in the pages that follow.

The usability of anything—physical product or service—is entirely situational. When this machine was out fighting fires, its usability was judged on other aspects than those that make it a neat place to play today. (Photo courtesy of shoutaboutcarolina.com.)

Does it do what I *want* it to do?
And what I *expect* it to do?

There are two sides to the usability coin: ease of use on one side and elegance and clarity on the other. Ease of use deals with physical properties ("It does what I *want* it to do."); elegance and clarity deals with the psychological properties ("It does what I

---

[1] On a recent visit to a former Soviet-bloc nation, a spotlessly uniformed 19-year old border guard, sporting big epaulettes and a big attitude, wouldn't let me *out* of the country (she didn't think my passport photo looked like me). It took three senior officials the better part of an hour to convince her to let me get on the plane. Clearly, my passport has a usability problem.

expect it to do."). That's why this book has been divided into two main sections. Within each of these sections, I outline five key issues I think you should consider. And within each of these sections, you find a lot of overlap.

Let me be the first to admit that the subject of usability can be sliced and diced sixteen ways to Sunday. So take any "rules" you hear—including my own suggestions—with a grain of salt. What I'm showing you here is merely one way that has proven successful in my own career. Please feel free to do whatever you think is right to make this information even more useful for yourself, your company, and your clients.

For three years, I was Professor of Usability and Design at the Instituto de Empresa Business School in Madrid, Spain. This was within the Master of Digital Marketing program. As far as I know, I was the only professor actually dealing with design aspects—most of the program dealt with entrepreneurship and similar business topics. What I am presenting here is pretty much what I also presented to my classes. And you know what? After a semester, many of my business students were doing usability studies that were as good as stuff I've seen from some professional usability evaluators. I figure if the methodology works with business students with no design background, most people ought to be able to carry out valuable usability improvements with a little practical guidance.

Why does it matter?

In the simplest terms, if a product works, you'll use it. If it doesn't work, you won't use it (although we do tolerate a lot of bad design decisions from iTunes, Facebook, and Microsoft). And because you usually have to buy something in order to use it, usability suddenly becomes an integral part of the online business case. Or at least it should be—particularly if you're giving people a free trial. But usability goes beyond basic ease of use. Remember, there are *two* sides to the usability coin—the other being psychological.

Let's say there are two pizza parlors in your neighborhood. The pizzas from both places are good. The prices are pretty much the same. But the owner of one pizza parlor barely acknowledges you when you place an order. The other greets you by name and makes you feel welcome.

Where would *you* go to buy a pizza?

Is this a service-design issue or a usability issue? I'd say both—because usability is directly related to user satisfaction.

Of course, I hear you cry, "But what is the *product*? Usability deals with the physical and psychological aspects of interaction with something. You just said so!" And you're right, of course—although your view is still narrower than necessary. (We'll work on that together.) Consider for a moment, as a customer, you prefer to "use" the pizza parlor with the good service. Right? So, service quality is therefore also part of the usability equation; the usability is not just about the quality of the product, the pizza, the packaging, and so on. One could argue that this makes service a product, too.

Not only do product and service usability complement each other, but ultimately, a bad experience with one element within a brand affects our willingness to get cozy with other elements. Let me tell you a quick story to illustrate why I think service and desirability need to be considered as usability elements, too.

My fancy dishwasher was recently repaired—covered by the warranty, thank goodness. The repairman explained that because our dishwasher had smashed so many glasses, the broken pieces had damaged the pump so the dishwasher no longer washed very well. Having spent hours changing pumps and filters and tubes—the innards of this thing look like a heart-lung machine—the friendly repairman diplomatically suggested that we shouldn't put broken glasses in the dishwasher and that our poor experience shouldn't reflect badly on the company in general.

Er . . . what? I don't wash broken glasses, I throw them out. My miserable *dishwasher* breaks my glasses—and doesn't even wash the bits and pieces very well (although it does let them ruin the pump).

Bottom line, my dishwasher is so mediocre (albeit expensive), that I have washed glasses by hand for more than a year. Will I buy another product from this well-known company? No. Does usability—in the broadest possible sense—affect the business case? You bet it does! To ignore usability is to lose money. It's as simple as that.

Who cares?

We all care! We may not immediately identify a problem as one of usability, but that doesn't matter. The problems related to usability are felt by one and all. Customers want to love your company; no one walks into a store or clicks on to a website if they *don't* want to deal with you.

When customers arrive, what is their mindset? Are they ready to deal with you or do they still need convincing? And if you can get them to deal with you the first time, will your products and services be so satisfying that they'll come back and deal with you again? Let's hope so.

Look at airlines. Despite all the many and varied loyalty programs, how loyal are travellers? Not very, according to industry analysts. Most passengers will tell you they just want to get from A to B in the easiest, cheapest way, more-or-less on time. (Hey, that's why the airlines have schedules, right?)

Sound reasonable? It should. But let's analyze this.

What is "cheapest"? What is "easiest"?

If the basic ticket is cheap, but it costs extra to reserve a seat next to your friend or spouse, costs extra to check a bag, costs extra to get a meal, and extra to do . . . whatever . . . is this still a "cheap" ticket?

Keep in mind, too, the more decisions we consumers need to make, the more difficult the degree of "usability." If the airline simply told us, "Don't fret. We'll take care of everything and it won't cost you extra," the airline would be making the usability easier, wouldn't you agree? And guess what, some people will even pay for this convenience!

Other companies have turned this around by making things *very* difficult for users. The idea here is that if a company goes out of its way *not* to provide good service, the products must be rock-bottom cheap. This is a trend we've seen in Europe the past decade or so, particularly at discount supermarkets. Here the aisles are cramped with unopened boxes of goods, there is little or no system as to how items are arranged, the product selection is haphazard, and there are always long lines at the solitary checkout.

What can we learn from this? That nothing is black and white in the usability industry! That's why you need to check out the fundamentals of this business because decisions related to usability directly affect profitability in most organizations. If you truly understand your options—and the consequences of your actions—you will make better decisions and earn more money for your company. Honest.

Make it useful, too!

You'd be surprised how many times usability and usefulness are confused. Here's a story:

Many years ago, I was scheduled to visit Copenhagen Airport at five in the morning to evaluate a sophisticated interactive audio interface. It was part of the first-class service on a B-747 for one of the world's most service-minded airlines. Although the system was incredible, no one seemed to be using it. During a short, pre-dawn layover, my task was to figure out why.

In those pre-iPod days, the idea that you had thousands of musical performances waiting in the arm of your seat was mind-boggling. First-class passengers could put together a custom playlist for their entire 12-hour journey between Europe and the airline's home hub in the Far East, which was the key to this innovative concept.

As it turned out, the system was both easy to use and highly intuitive, but it had one major flaw: Who would want to spend his or her time putting together a one-time only playlist? Although the interface was extremely *usable*, it wasn't necessarily *useful* to passengers who just wanted to relax in luxury while winging their way across a continent or two.

My suggestion was simple: reinstate the classic categories—rock, jazz, classic, easy listening, and so on. Press one button and let the machine take over. I also suggested a simple Reject button so passengers could move on to the next selection if they didn't like what was playing. And guess what? Passengers started to use the new system—and liked it!

The lesson to be learned here is that just because you *can* do something, it doesn't mean you *should* do something. Too many applications, intranet features, and pages and pages of meaningless web content have been created because "someone might want this." As Alan Cooper, creator of the persona concept and one of our industry's true pioneers once remarked, "When you hear 'someone might want this' you know you're about to hear a really bad design decision."

So, please, I hope you will design apps that people *will* use. Build intranet features that really *do* help people work smarter. And design a 100-page website that has *killer content* instead of one with 500 pages that are all gravy but no meat.

Bogo Vatovec's three-stage usability plan

One evening, my good friend, Bogo, explained this model over a beer. He says there are three stages to implementing usability in any organization:

1. Nobody talks about usability.
2. Everybody talks about usability.
3. Nobody talks about usability.

The first stage is obvious (well, not to you because you picked up this book). Shockingly, most companies still seem to ignore usability although most do give it lip service. During the second stage, though, some outside expert has held a series of inspirational workshops and the whole company is talking about how usability is going to change their world. The third stage is tricky because it can go two ways:

The best way is that nobody talks about usability because everyone takes it for granted. It has become part of the project development process. It's part of the business plan. It's built into the system and the hearts and minds of the people who work within this system.

That's the good version.

The not-so-good version is that as soon as the expensive consultant leaves, people forget what all the fuss was about. This seems to be the more typical result, which is also one of the reasons why I decided to write this book. Even a lone individual can make a real change after he or she catches on to a few simple ideas.

Bogo Vatovec's three-step usability plan is so simple, we sketched the first version on the back of a beer mat. The third step is the tricky one and can either be wildly successful or a total failure. It's up to you to steer things in the right direction.

You don't need a big budget

About 10 or 15 years ago, running a formal usability test for a website meant writing out a test protocol, recruiting a half-dozen test subjects, plunking these folks down, one at a time, in a room that looked very similar to a police interrogation room—with the client and designers scrutinizing the test subjects' every move from the other side of a one-way mirror.

Well, we've learned a lot these past years and, although usability problems still abound, we've stopped making a lot of the mistakes we made 10 years ago. That's because we have some fairly well-defined "best practices" and some pretty solid design patterns from which to choose when putting together a website. That also means usability testing, at least for websites, has become fairly commoditized and therefore cheaper. And tiny webcams have dramatically reduced the need for creepy one-way mirrors and a formal test lab.

But what about mobile apps? What about industrial interfaces? How do you test stuff that you can't even move into a usability lab, such as the controls for a wastewater-treatment facility? Or the dashboard for a car?

If you're going to do true usability testing—which is still a very good idea—you have to do special projects "in the field" for the most part. But here's the cool part: If you take these principles to heart and start thinking in terms of usability, you'll be amazed at the number of problems you can avoid just by using a little common sense. Let me be completely honest here—very few industrial companies actually conduct formal usability tests on their designs. They should, but most don't. Throughout this book I share some of the weirder examples I've experienced.

One of the biggest challenges in most companies is to get a budget to test the usability of something that has already been launched, shipped, or commissioned—from websites to wastewater-treatment plants. That's why each of the chapters in this book ends with a simple checklist that highlights some of the typical problems to watch for. If you spot something, fix it; you probably won't need to run a formal test, yet you'll be making your product a whole lot better.

Remember, too, that when dealing with interactive media, you are part of a *process*, not a *project*. In other words, there should be an opportunity to make small, incremental improvements. That said, if the folks controlling the purse-strings in your company only see things as fixed-term projects, your chances of getting any kind of budget for usability testing is pretty slim. So check out those checklists!

I suspect that a lot of industrial interfaces are designed by engineering teams who have never really thought about usability. Did you know there is still debate whether pressing a single button during a reactor test inadvertently triggered the Chernobyl nuclear explosion? If you're part of a team designing behind-the-scenes equipment, here's your chance to do some real good.

A note about the non-English website examples

I live in Copenhagen, Denmark. And because my company is international, I see sites and apps in lots of languages other than English and I want to share some of these with you. Don't be nervous. Whatever I want to illustrate will not require you to rush to Google Translate. Think of these sites as being "greeked" as they say in the ad biz (when real text is not yet available, the art director pastes *Latin* text into a design to make the ad look realistic). I don't think language will be a problem—and it goes to show that many of the issues are fairly universal.

I'm messing with your brain

One of the best usability books I've ever read was written by my friend Steve Krug. It's called *Don't Make Me Think* (New Riders, 2005). Why do I mention Steve? Well, it's because his book speaks to the needs of the user—"don't make me think." The "me" refers to the user. But if *you* are to make a useful contribution to your company, your team, yourself, you *must* think. I'm going to share ideas with you that will *make* you think.

Unfortunately, after you start thinking about this stuff, it's hard to stop. You'll soon find that your family will no longer go to restaurants with you because you'll find 16 ways to improve the service (and seek out the manager after the meal). You'll look for the link to webmaster@wherever.com before you look for the shopping cart. You'll be redesigning your lemon squeezer instead of making lemonade for your kids. It's like a picture of a Rubin vase, where you either see a goblet or two faces. After the two images have been pointed out, you can't help but see them both.

Granted, it's a tough job, but someone has to do it. If you aren't up to the task, stop reading *now*. Put the book back on the shelf. Give it to your worst enemy. Because I am certain it *will* make you think.

In the introduction to *The Pre-History of The Far Side* (Andrews and McMeel, 1989), Gary Larson, the creator of these bizarrely entertaining cartoons, tells us: "That's the story. Of course, I don't know how interesting any of this really is, but now you've got it in your brain cells so you're stuck with it."

If you read on, you're "stuck with it."

This famous optical illusion was introduced by the Danish psychologist Edgar Rubin in 1915. It contains two very different images. Can you see them? If not, keep looking. When you do, it will be impossible for you not to see both of them in the future. Thinking about usability works the same way: After you catch on to what to look for, you'll never be able to ignore it again. (Photo courtesy of John Smithson, the Wikipedia Project.)

OTHER BOOKS
YOU MIGHT LIKE

Effecting change in any organization can be tough. If you want some help and inspiration in getting your company to work better, here are a few books I've found particularly useful:

> *The Secret Handshake: Mastering The Politics Of The Business Inner Circle*, Kathleen Kelley Reardon, Ph.D., Currency Doubleday, 2000

> *Switch: How To Change Things When Change Is Hard*, Chip and Dan Heath, Random House Business Books, 2011

> *Dealing with Difficult People. Results-Driven Manager Series*, Harvard Business School Press, 2005

THINGS TO
GOOGLE

> Bogo Vatovec
> Alan Cooper
> Usability plan
> Service design

Part One
Ease of Use

These first five chapters are about physical parameters, which basically ensure that something does what you want it to do. Buttons, controls, and other response mechanisms are there to help you accomplish your task, and they might include functions and features that may even anticipate your needs and habits. In short, these things make stuff easy to use.

You might think that this idea is something of a no-brainer, but it isn't. Despite all the lip service to "user-friendliness," a depressing number of programs and products are still pretty UN-friendly. Throughout the next five chapters, I'm going to show you how well-meaning design doesn't always lead to well-functioning stuff.

What's in this part?

This part covers the following aspects of "ease of use":

- ▶ Functional (it actually works)
- ▶ Responsive (I know it's working; it knows where it's working)
- ▶ Ergonomic (I can easily see, click, poke, twist, and turn stuff)
- ▶ Convenient (everything is right where I need it)
- ▶ Foolproof (the designer helps me to not make mistakes or break stuff)

I have this goofy hope that when you see this list, you will say to yourself, "Yeah. That makes sense. What's the big deal?" But to illustrate my point, please take a moment to go to your favorite website. Click around for a couple of minutes while thinking about these issues. Can you see something that could be improved based on anything on this list? I bet you can! Welcome to the world of usability.

Chapter One

Functional

Flick a light switch and you expect the lights to come on. Turn the key in the ignition and you expect your car to start. You expect your refrigerator to be cold, your oven to be hot. These are all functional interactions. If things don't work at this very basic level, then it really doesn't matter much how beautiful a design may be. So what better place to start a discussion of usability than with functionality?

Please keep in mind that there will be some overlap between the discussion of functionality and other issues in the "ease-of-use" part of this book. For now, I'm concentrating on the "works/doesn't work" aspects of usability and design, although I revisit some of the things discussed here throughout the book.

Delicious Spanish dessert at a trendy Madrid restaurant. But how did they expect me to use the very round spoon to get in the corners of the very square bowl? I used my fingers to circumvent this amusing functional failure.

In one of the most technologically sophisticated environments—the modern airport—a chock of wood with a rope attached is still the preferred method for keeping planes parked correctly. An elegantly simple and highly functional solution.

The three keys to functionality

Just for a moment, consider the faucet on your sink. When you turn the taps, you expect water to come out. You want to be able to easily adjust the temperature. And if you want very hot or very cold water, you don't want to have to run the water for a long time.

In more general terms, these same three functions also sum up the basic needs on a website:

▶ The buttons and links must work when you click them.

▶ The navigation must be responsive.

▶ The processing speed must be acceptable.

A frightening number of websites, apps, services, and so on fail for these very three reasons. So do some faucets . . . the same generic issues guide many products in the physical world.

This frying pan is so poorly balanced that it can't fry anything—unless you hold up the handle (or fry really heavy eggs). Functional deficiencies can appear in very strange ways; the average person looking at this utensil in a store won't think to check the balance, so the designers should do it for them.

From click to conversion: making sure the buttons work

You're probably thinking, "Hey, broken buttons should be fixed. This is a no-brainer." And you're right. Amazingly, broken buttons are a bigger problem than you may think. And I don't mean only links that may have broken, but also basic mechanisms that simply don't work. Let me tell you a story.

My daughter-in-law wanted some earrings that were available on a jewelry store's website. I found the earrings and clicked "Put in basket." But when I went to check out, my basket was empty. Assuming I had made a mistake of some kind (because this problem was simply too absurd to show up on a professional e-commerce site), I repeated the procedure—and got the same useless result. Out of curiosity, I tried to put other products in my basket. Nothing made it to the check-out. Something was clearly broken.

When I called the store to order the earrings, I was told that practically all of their business is through their offline outlets. "Our sales via our website are pretty much nonexistent." Duh. Of course sales are nonexistent if it is physically impossible to buy something, which forces people to call or visit the store in person.

 The page cannot be found

The page you are looking for might have been removed, had its name changed, or is temporarily unavailable.

Please try the following:

- If you typed the page address in the Address bar, make sure that it is spelled correctly.
- Open the httpd.apache.org home page, and then look for links to the information you want.
- Click the ⇐ Back button to try another link.
- Click 🔍 Search to look for information on the Internet.

HTTP 404 - File not found
Internet Explorer

Dead link? Server down? Something else? If your web analytics program is telling you that your 404 - Page Not Found error is getting a lot of page views, you need to investigate immediately.

As we spoke, I realized that the company had no clue as to *why* online sales were nil. Because the company didn't really take e-commerce seriously, no one at the company was actually looking very closely at the functionality of the website.

What *does* it cost a company when people can't deal with a company online? If no other channels exist (i.e. a business is only available online) then the cost will be significant, but then again, online-only companies probably look carefully at how the website is performing and catch problems very quickly. It's when alternative channels are available (a physical store, for example) that businesses tend to neglect the online presence, as the jewelry store did.

If the attitude of the site owner is "Well, we have a site because everyone else has one. . ." then you are bound to run into problems like this. Of course, these kinds of things are usually easy to fix, but you do have to find them first.

Browser wars, hardware headaches

Obviously, to check the functionality of any screen-based interactive product, the first thing to do is to click through it. For websites, various tools such as Google Analytics also help you spot dead links and such. But what you really want to look for are navigational elements that are programmed wrong so that they lead you to the wrong page, or even the same page (yes, this happens a lot).

You should also download a couple of different browsers to see that everything works equally well across a variety of tools. At a minimum, check your site in the following:

- ▶ Internet Explorer
- ▶ Safari
- ▶ Firefox
- ▶ Opera

You may also find that various small interactive elements, such as in-screen audio or video controls and animations, will simply not work across all platforms. For example, widgets programmed in Flash (an Adobe animation tool) will not display on some Apple products (notoriously the iPad[1]). If interactive elements are essential to your site, check their performance on popular operating systems for:

- ▶ Smartphones
- ▶ Tablets
- ▶ Laptops
- ▶ Smart TVs

[1]In the biography by Walter Isaacson (Simon & Schuster, 2011), Steve Jobs states that Flash technology used up too much of the iPad's precious battery power in relation to other programming options. Hmm. Legitimate technical consideration or business vendetta? The jury is still out.

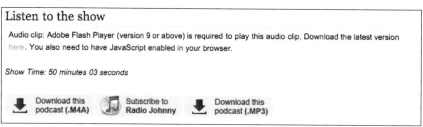

On most devices, a small Flash graphic enables people to control an audio podcast (top). But an iPad does not display Flash, so these controls disappear, rendering the website unusable. Curiously, my iPad was nice enough to tell me where I could download the software it refuses to acknowledge (bottom).

Don't sweat the home page. Fine-tune your forms.

I spend a depressing amount of time in design meetings listening to people fret about the home page of a website. Yet the home page is arguably the *least* important page. Sure, the home page gives you an opportunity to spell out the big picture—what the site is about—and display a range of informational/functional options available to the visitor. But in truth, the better you design this online welcome mat, the less time visitors will spend on it. That's because they'll quickly spot the link that gets them where they want to go. Moreover, some people access your site from a search engine that leads them to a page far deeper into your site. Chances are that many folks don't even see your home page.

From a business perspective, your home page probably isn't where you create online conversions—which is almost always a top priority—getting people to order your product, sign up for your newsletter, download a document, submit a blog comment, or even just send you an e-mail. Conversions don't always involve money (although many do). That said, most conversions require visitors to fill in an online form of some kind. Therefore, if you are going to fine-tune any pages on your site, you should concentrate on your forms.

Form problems are related to those of broken buttons because something on the site is preventing your visitors from interacting with you in the intended manner. However, as opposed to broken buttons that get in the way of *all* visitors, most form-design problems are much more difficult to spot because the form undoubtedly works for at least one group of users—the one on which the original design team focused.

Four keys to creating functional forms

Although I get into other aspects of form design later on, in terms of functionality, there are four things you need to keep in mind:

▶ People have to be able to provide the information you are demanding.

▶ Inflexible input formats greatly increase the chances of form failure.

▶ The need for interdependent forms and logins also increase the chances of failure.

▶ Instructions that are misleading are a great way to frustrate your users.

Obviously, there are other issues, such as the security of a password, how the on-screen messages are phrased, whether the layout is easy to understand, and so on. But one thing at a time. . . .

Required fields

A *field* is a section of a form—one of those little rectangular areas in which you can type something. The term stems from database design, but it is now used pretty broadly by the design community. Often, when a form is designed, specific fields are marked in some way, usually with an asterisk (*) to indicate that the visitor has to fill something out in order to complete the form—a so-called required field. Alternatively, the field may simply represent supplementary information that the site owner would like to collect, but which isn't absolutely necessary in order to complete a transaction. In fact, within the European Union, it is actually illegal to require a visitor to provide this kind of "nice-to-have" data. Curiously, when I recently signed up for a free e-paper on a major U.S. publisher's website, I was required to provide credit-card details! But I digress. . . .

If you are a designer working on a website designed primarily for visitors from the United States, it is tempting to make *State* a required field when folks are asked to provide an address. And if you also are catering to visitors from Canada, you probably want to use more encompassing wording such as *State/Province*.

As it happens, I live in Denmark—imagine an entire country that's no bigger than Houston or Miami in terms of population. Not surprisingly, Denmark doesn't have "states." Actually, most of Europe doesn't have states, provinces, or regions. That means if you make this a required field, there is no way for a large part of the world to complete this form.

This is one of those situations where a programmer or designer may create something that works perfectly well for one group of visitors, but ends in catastrophe for others. Because most of these state/province fields actually have a drop-down list of options, it would certainly help Europeans if "None" was an option. And what about the Australians, who *do* have states, but not the ones on the American lists? One solution to this problem might be to simply ask for the country *before* asking for other address information and have the form adjust itself as needed. (If your programming team thinks this is simply too much bother, then you really need to ask yourself why you're wasting time thinking about usability at all.)

Anyway, when testing a form, make sure folks can reasonably provide all of the information needed to complete the form. I am firmly convinced that this is without question the single greatest reason for conversion failures.

You fill out this entry card before you enter the Russian Federation. But unless you are Russian, the concept of a "patronymic" will probably be something of a mystery to you. Hence, this form is confusing to most foreigners.

Forms and business rules

Field validations help the computer make sure it is getting data that it understands and can file appropriately in its database. They are there to check syntax, make sure there are enough numbers in a credit-card number, and so on. The problem is that these rules are invisible to the user, which means that the opportunities for error are enormous.

For example, if you want users to type in a credit-card number, some folks type in spaces between the four-digit segments; others just type in the 16-digit number in one long string. If your validation rules are inflexible, only accepting one of these input options, you're going to frustrate a lot of people. Obviously, the system needs to get 16 digits, not counting spaces. That's a legitimate requirement. But fussing about the spacing is nonsense. It's easy to program things in a more flexible way, and you should make sure someone does so.

Telephone numbers, addresses, postal codes, dates, and all kinds of data (generally numerical) tend to cause problems. Even when I can get a site to accept that I don't have a state, I often find that it still won't accept my four-digit postal code or the Danish spelling of my street name (Strandøre).

When testing the business rules, the idea is not to see what works, but to try and break the system. Ask your family to take a shot at it. This is a remarkably effective way to spot some basic problems.

Interdependent forms

For some reason, online ticketing sites for movie theaters where I live let me choose my seats and get fairly far along in the purchase process before they suddenly ask me to provide user-registration info—a username and password. Honestly, I go to the movies so infrequently that any registration information I may have submitted on a previous visit has long since been forgotten. And if I don't have it, I must interrupt my task to complete another task that seems more for the benefit of the site owner than for me.

Recently, my wife booked tickets so she could take our granddaughter to *Disney on Ice*. Eventually, she located a ticketing website, found good seats, and was about to pay ,when she was suddenly required to register her personal data with the site owner. Déjà vu! What made this particular situation interesting was that the website gave her just five minutes to complete this task or she would lose the seats and have to start over. Alas, the registration process took almost 10 minutes due to slow servers and other technical limitations. All in all, it took her almost 30 minutes to book the two tickets. She was furious, vowing never again to use this miserable website—and by extension, was mad at the Disney organization that actually had nothing to do with the operation of the ticketing website. (There's a service-design lesson to be learned here.)

Naturally, some interdependent forms, such as several sequential pages in a shopping cart, are not nearly as odious. The problem occurs when a website breaks a sequential process by asking the user to do something else before continuing on his or her journey. The perception of a user experience is formed as folks move along a path leading from one interaction to the next. Don't get in the way.

In short, if you have two different forms that need to be completed, make sure folks see these in the appropriate order. And for goodness sake, give folks enough time to fill out both forms satisfactorily before you time them out!

Happily, the login page for Amazon turns up early in the customer journey, so getting through the check-out is easy and straightforward.

Instructions and functionality

I'm always amazed at websites and other stuff that ask me to do something very specific and then complain when I do exactly what I've been asked to do. This often happens when the person who wrote the instructions (or documentation) has no contact with the designer/programmer and vice versa. Here are two quick examples.

Years ago, I had a crazy VCR made by the German manufacturer Saba. I wish I still had it because it was a classic example of an over-designed machine—there were no fewer than 46 buttons on the front panel! About half of them were labeled in German, and the other half in English. The main power, for example, was indicated in English: Off/On. But the timer function was labeled with the German equivalent: Auf/Zu.

Already here you can see that there is a basic cognitive problem, particularly if the user doesn't happen to speak German. But to make matters worse, the rather huge instruction book that came with the rather huge machine often reversed things. For example, it insisted I push Zu to turn on the main power and On to activate the timer, which was the exact reverse of the button legends printed on the machine itself. Needless to say, it took a bit of experimentation to get the beast to work.

The lesson is this: When testing stuff, follow whatever instructions you have been given *to the letter*! If the instructions don't work or don't make sense, you are going to run into functional problems, so be on the lookout for these kinds of issues and fix them. It's also a good idea to keep everything in the same language. Think about this the next time you visit an international website that mixes and matches languages on the same page.

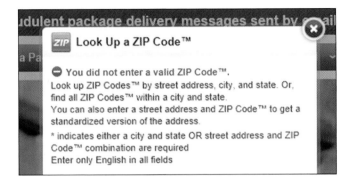

The United States Postal Service has a convenient ZIP Code™ finder. But why did the designers make ZIP Code a required field? This is precisely the information people are looking for!

The second example I'd like to share is from a form on the Brazilian Embassy's website that asked me for a date (I was applying for a visa). The instructions in parentheses next to the form field told me specifically to enter my data using the following format: dd/mm/yyyy (with slashes). However, for reasons known only to the backend developers, the date would only be accepted if I typed in: ddmmyyyy (no slashes). It took quite some time to figure out what was going wrong here when the site refused to accept my submission.

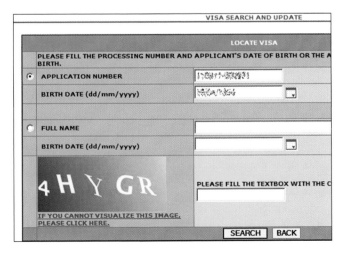

Although this website form from the Brazilian Embassy in Copenhagen tells me exactly how I should enter a date, the business rules for this site actually insist on a very different format without slashes: ddmmyyyy. This is as confusing as it is frustrating.

Honestly, it is a fairly simple matter to get a database to ignore the slashes, dashes, spaces, and anything else people might type in this field. And to actually *ask* for a particular format and then reject the data is a sure-fire recipe for disaster.

Navigation: Getting folks where they want to go

The second of my three main functionality points deals with the responsiveness of navigation, which is closely related to the third point—processing speed. There are actually two sides to this issue. One side deals with the cognitive feedback from a site or device, which I talk about in the next chapter. The other deals with speed and efficiency, which is what I'd like to talk about now.

My crappy new TV

I recently bought a cheapo LED TV to put in our spare bedroom. It is very shiny and skinny and has a wonderfully sharp picture. But it has the reaction time of an anesthetized turtle. Each time I punch up a new channel, the TV takes five to eight seconds to respond. Needless to say, it is virtually impossible to zap around looking for something interesting to watch. Today, my family does not let me use it unless I have a *TV Guide* in front of me; they are convinced I will die of apoplexy if I don't have a precise viewing plan *before* I turn the thing on.

But guess what? It turns out I'm not the only impatient person on this planet. When it comes to websites and conversion factors, there is a growing body of proof that the faster a page responds to your request, the better the conversion. Google and Amazon have both documented how cutting response times by as little as half a second can provide major conversion improvements.

One of the really good articles on the subject is by Steve Souders. Even though it was written a while back (2009), it certainly indicates a clear trend. For example, when Shopzilla sped things up from approximately seven seconds to two seconds, they experienced a 25 percent increase in page views, a 7 to 12 percent increase in revenue, and a 50 percent reduction in hardware. Suffice it to say, this is an important issue. Google the title "Velocity and the Bottom Line" if you want all the details.

As to testing any stuff you may have, if you think it seems slow, I guarantee you others will think that it's even slower. So figure out if there is something you can do to improve the situation. Compressing the file size of photos and graphics is a really good place to start and can be done by anyone with access to a simple graphics program such as Photoshop. (By the way, the rule of thumb is that whatever you feel is the *least* acceptable quality, you can probably shave the size just a bit more. Don't look at the two photos side-by-side or you will invariably make your file too big. Judge the web-optimized photo or graphic on its own merits.)

Unless you're actually programming your stuff, there probably isn't much else you can do directly, but at least you know enough to complain to the proper team within your organization. Remember, too, that Internet connectivity in some geographic areas and on some mobile networks can be pretty slow. Speeding things up invariably means streamlining or eliminating some of the the eye-candy.

Understand your goals and keep them in focus

It's easy to lose sight of the goals of your stuff. What is the purpose? Why did we start this project? Are we meeting the goals of the user? (If we aren't, we'll probably never meet our own business goals.) Your answers to these questions ultimately reflect the functional requirements your stuff needs to demonstrate if it is to be successful.

As a project develops, there is a sad tendency to add features that actually get in the way of what you want to accomplish. This is what happens when someone has a neat idea, and that neat idea becomes more interesting to work on than the more mundane tasks, such as designing forms that work.

I'm going to assume for a moment that you already have some project you want to examine from a usability point of view. There are two questions you should be asking yourself:

▶ What are the goals?

▶ What conversions are we measuring to see if we meet these goals?

For example, the goal of a household thermostat could be to help people maintain a comfortable temperature. Or the goal of an online CD site might be to sell CDs and related items. Or the goal of the Boy Scouts website might be to encourage ethics and leadership.

And as to conversion metrics, the thermostat might be judged on how infrequently it needs to be adjusted. The CD site could be measured in terms of sales. And the Scouts could look at the number of new sign-ups and new scout troops being formed.

Whatever functionality you are evaluating, make sure it truly supports your goals and facilitates your conversions.

A true story about a fairy tale

Why do we tell our kids fairy tales? Not lies, but stories by the Brothers Grimm, Mother Goose, Hans Christian Andersen, and others. Well, often, there are moral lessons to be learned or interesting descriptions of ancient customs. A lot of them are just hugely entertaining stories.

Although this book of fairy tales may be cute, it completely fails to convey any of the moral, historical, and ethical lessons of the original stories. The functionality got in the way of some worthwhile goals. Don't let this happen to your products and services.

It was with a sense of disappointment that I came across a strange book a couple of years ago, *Mixed Up Fairy Tales* by Hilary Robinson and Nick Sharratt. Here, about a dozen stories (Jack and the Beanstalk, Puss in Boots, Cinderella, and so on) were presented in split-page form so that children could combine any four bits of plot and still make something that made sense grammatically, if not logically.

The back cover provides a typical example:

"Do you know the tale of Aladdin who climbed up a beanstalk and found a helping
of porridge at the top?"

Cute as this idea is, it completely fails to help children understand these stories. In fact, I even had trouble trying to put together the right bits for some of them. Incidentally, I once saw a restaurant menu made in the same way. As a result, you could create your own page describing your meal, but it was very difficult to gain an overview of the available dishes.

Both of these spiral-bound volumes struck me as perfect examples of counterproductive functionality. My advice? Without a clear set of design priorities, it's easy to let yourself be swept away by so-called "creative" solutions.

Watch out for counterproductive creativity! The Danish architect, Poul Henningsen, once said of the iconic bentwood chair from Thonet, "By making this chair five times as expensive, three times heavier, half as comfortable, and only a fraction as beautiful, an architect can make a good name for himself." (Photo from *Kritisk Revy*, no. 4, 1927)

Functionality can change over time

We've all seen overfilled trash cans in public places. When they are overfilled, they cease to work; you can't put trash in an overfilled receptacle. Is this a functionality problem? Yes, if the container is undersized in relation to the trash it is expected to handle. But it could also be that this is a service-design problem—that the receptacle needs to be emptied more often.

When evaluating your stuff, keep in mind that a problem related to function may actual stem from something other than the physical design or technical configuration.

Remember, too, to give folks a warning if something might "break." For example, if a first-time customer cannot place an order for more than 100 dollars, it would be a good idea to tell folks *before* they go on wild shopping sprees. Another example could be e-commerce sites that have items that are not available in all markets. Again, tell folks *before* they order something.

These trash cans at London's Heathrow Airport are unusable. But is this a physical design problem? Perhaps they just need to be emptied more often, which would make this a service-design issue.

A complaint is a gift

A few days ago, I discovered a functional error on the www.amazon.co.uk site that prevented the sale of a simple digital clock to Denmark: "This product is not available in your location." Wow, how odd considering that the seller shipped internationally and both the United Kingdom and Denmark are members of the European Union and thus not subject to internal trade barriers. I wrote to Amazon and the problem was corrected within a couple of hours. Well done, Amazon!

Make sure someone is paying attention to the feedback users are giving your company. Don't just let these messages pile up on a mail server somewhere. If people take the time to tell you about a problem, the very least you can do is acknowledge their help and try to make things better. As my old mentor, service guru Claus Møller used to say, "a complaint is a gift."

▶ THE DONATION THAT COULDN'T BE MADE
A TALE FROM THE TRENCHES

FOR MORE THAN 60 YEARS, my family has supported an American civil-rights organization, the NAACP. In early 2011, it came time for me to take over the family's charitable duties.

So far, so good. The NAACP has a big donation link right there on the home page.

The website gave me a direct link from the home page to a donation page. Great. I clicked. I then tried to fill out the form. Not so great.

MORE >

▶ **THE DONATION THAT COULDN'T BE MADE**
A TALE FROM THE TRENCHES

IT'S BEEN A GREAT 2010.
HELP US MAKE 2011 EVEN BETTER!

With the help of loyal supporters like you, 2010 has been an amazing year for the NAACP. Among the top items that we accomplished together were:

- Helping prevent the state of Texas from rewriting America's racial history in its textbooks
- Calling attention to the racist elements of the Tea Party movement, and helping force out racist Tea Party leader Mark Williams
- Help narrow the discriminatory gap between crack and cocaine sentencing
- Helping secure $1.25 billion for upwards of 70,000 black farmers in a settlement with the U.S. Department of Agriculture
- Supporting the Scott sisters in their bid for justice in Mississippi

But we need your help to continue the fight in 2011, to make America a better place for citizens of all colors.

last name
Reiss
suffix

address
Strandøre 15

city
Copenhagen
state/region/province

zip
2100
email address

phone number

And I start filling out the form. . . .

First, the site insisted that I provide the name of a U.S. state. As my parents had lived in Florida, I used this. Good choice as the site then complained about my four-digit Danish ZIP Code. So, I used the old Florida ZIP. After much fussing, I also managed to get the site to accept a telephone number it liked. Actually, I'm not sure it's even legal to make a phone number a required piece of information on a U.S. site; it certainly isn't within the European Community for this kind of transaction.

With the help of loyal supporters like you, 2010 has been an amazing year for the NAACP. Among the top items that we accomplished together were:

- Helping prevent the state of Texas from rewriting America's racial history in its textbooks
- Calling attention to the racist elements of the Tea Party movement, and helping force out racist Tea Party leader Mark Williams
- Help narrow the discriminatory gap between crack and cocaine sentencing
- Helping secure $1.25 billion for upwards of 70,000 black farmers in a settlement with the U.S. Department of Agriculture
- Supporting the Scott sisters in their bid for justice in Mississippi

But we need your help to continue the fight in 2011, to make America a better place for citizens of all colors.

Donate to the NAACP today by simply filling out the credit card contribution form to your right.

last name
Reiss
suffix

address
Strandøre 15

city
Copenhagen
state/region/province
required field

zip
not a valid zip code
2100
email address

phone number
required field

Amount

What do they mean this isn't a valid ZIP??? It is in Denmark! And I don't have a state. And they also want my phone number. . . . Yikes.

THE DONATION THAT COULDN'T BE MADE
A TALE FROM THE TRENCHES

My next step was to give the site my credit-card information. To my surprise, this was accepted—but only for a minute. The site then informed me that the billing information for my card (which the site had gathered from who-knows-where) did not match the address I had provided. Well, of course not! The site wouldn't let me give my proper address! So much for my attempt to game the system. Obviously, the site wants to make sure my card wasn't stolen, but hey, a lot of cards *aren't* registered at the same address as the user—corporate cards, debit cards, and so on. This particular automatic security measure just doesn't work very effectively.

HELP US MAKE 2011 EVEN BETTER!

With the help of loyal supporters like you, 2010 has been an amazing year for the NAACP. Among the top items that we accomplished together were:

- Helping prevent the state of Texas from rewriting America's racial history in its textbooks
- Calling attention to the racist elements of the Tea Party movement, and helping force out racist Tea Party leader Mark Williams
- Help narrow the discriminatory gap between crack and cocaine sentencing
- Helping secure $1.25 billion for upwards of 70,000 black farmers in a settlement with the U.S. Department of Agriculture
- Supporting the Scott sisters in their bid for justice in Mississippi

But we need your help to continue the fight in 2011, to make America a better place for citizens of all colors.

Donate to the NAACP today by simply filling out the credit card contribution form to your right.

last name
Reiss

suffix

address
Strandøre 15

city
Copenhagen

state/region/province
Florida

zip
33156

email address

phone number
not a valid phone number
+45 20 12

So I start gaming the system—giving it any information that will get this process moving. . . .

Anyway, having failed miserably to give away my money, I was surprised a couple of days later when the NAACP thanked me for joining. Even so, the donation never turned up on my bank account, only the organization's unsolicited e-mails in my inbox. I don't honestly know if I am now a member or not.

At some point, I'll write a check, put it in an envelope, and send it off. When I get an American checkbook. When I find the NAACP's address. If I remember to do so. . . .

MORE >

► **THE DONATION THAT COULDN'T BE MADE**
A TALE FROM THE TRENCHES

WWW.NAACP.ORG

Error Processing Contribution

Your credit card contribution could not be authorized.

This could be because:

1. You accidentally entered your credit card number or expiration date incorrectly.
2. The address you provided does not match the billing address of your credit card.

<< Click here to edit and resubmit your contribution.

If the contribution still does not process, contact your credit card company.

What??? It seems the NAACP doesn't want my money anyway. And where did the site get my billing information? And why do they make this sound like it's all my fault?

TEN FUNCTIONAL THINGS TO WATCH OUT FOR

1. What are the goals of your stuff? Do you have a clear idea? If not, spend a quiet half hour thinking this through and then test the tasks involved to see if you can actually accomplish what you set out to do. (You may identify several goals and related tasks. Check them all.)

2. Do you have a form people have to fill out? Are you asking for information people might not have, such as a fax number?

3. If people are interrupted during an interaction with your stuff, will they be able to resume their tasks when they return? If not, what can you change to make things easier?

4. Can you think of any "edge" cases? What if someone doesn't live in your country? What if the person doesn't have a five-digit ZIP or a seven-digit phone number or needs both letters and numbers to provide a postal code? Will the visitor be able to fill out your form? If not, can you eliminate the hurdles?

5. Are your forms "forgiving"? Or are the back-end business rules dictating overly rigid input patterns?

6. If something doesn't work, are you giving users an alternative course of action? For example, is there a dedicated e-mail address or phone number to supplement an online contact form?

7. If you put something in a shopping basket/cart on an e-commerce site, is the item really getting placed in the cart? Can you complete the check-out process? Can your mother?

8. Will your stuff become less functional over time (like an overfilled trash can)? Do you actually have a functional problem or is this a question of redesigning a process or service?

9. Does your stuff work across all browser platforms? Does it work well on different devices (smartphones, tablets, laptops)? Pay particular attention to mission-critical stuff such as online forms, video and audio controls, and dashboard-type widgets.

10. Are your photos and graphics taking too long to load? Is it possible to optimize them to reduce the size of the individual files?

OTHER BOOKS
YOU MIGHT LIKE

Here are some of the books that I think deal effectively with basic functionality issues (although not exclusively—there's lots of good stuff here):

▶ *Defensive Design for the Web: How to Improve Error Messages, Help, Forms, and Other Crisis Points.* Matthew Linderman with Jason Fried (37 signals), New Riders, 2004

▶ *Forms that Work: Designing Web Forms for Usability.* Caroline Jarrett, Gerry Gaffney, Morgan Kaufmann, 2009

▶ *Web Forms Design: filling in the blanks.* Luke Wroblewski, Rosenfeld Media, 2008

THINGS TO
GOOGLE

▶ Defensive design

▶ Forms design

▶ Online conversion

▶ Service functionality

▶ Velocity and the bottom line

Chapter Two

Responsive

Watch and listen to two people engaged in conversation, and you'll notice one does the talking, the other the listening. They'll take turns reversing these roles, repeating the pattern until the conversation is over. You'll also notice how the listener is sending discreet signals in response to the speaker. Some of these responses are visual—a nod of the head, a frown, a smile, a hand gesture. Other responses are auditory—a laugh, a grunt, a "Hmm," or some other noise. Occasionally, the response is tactile—a pat on the back, for example. In all instances, sensory feedback is a critical part of effective communications—and to good usability.

Of course, sensory feedback in areas other than conversation can include any of our five senses; we smell the fresh-brewed coffee and know it's ready to drink; parents put bitter drops on their children's fingers to keep them from biting their nails. But whatever response mechanisms are present in our stuff, they must be appropriate, timely, and understood—for example, having our phone vibrate when we switch it to silent during a meeting.

When response mechanisms are inappropriate or lacking entirely, usability invariably suffers—imagine a phone that *only* vibrates and is unable to ring. Sound silly? You'll be surprised at the number of times appropriate responses are not provided during the course of your day— from something simple, such as the baristas forgetting to tell you that your cappuccino is ready, to something more complicated, such as a lack of confirmation after you've bought something online.

The myth of two-way communication

Honestly, I'm not convinced that two-way communication really exists. Oh, I know that we talk about it and the dictionary definition of the telephone explains that the device provides "real-time, two-way communication." But when we start dissecting things, it strikes me that most effective communications follow a fairly predictable, highly linear pattern:

1. Action
2. Acknowledgement
3. New action

The acknowledgement functions as a "receipt" that an action has been noted by the other party. It's a critical part of the communication process. These are the responses I mentioned at the start of the chapter—the grunts and smiles and gestures that listeners use to acknowledge they have heard what was said.

We humans rely a lot on this feedback. For example, when we speak on the phone, if we don't hear appropriate "receipts" from the person on the other end, we invariably ask "Hello? Are you still there?" The noises made by the listener on the other end of the line are both useful and reassuring.

With these thoughts in mind, let's see how responsive elements can improve usability—or break it when they're used poorly.

Three traditional keys to responsiveness

You can divide responsiveness into three broad groups:

▶ **Invitational tricks:** Movement designed to attract the eye and signal that something good is about to happen. Examples of this include banner ads, or even static, highly contextual "see also" links on a web page—the stuff usually displayed in the right-hand column.

▶ **Transitional techniques:** The here-and-now responses to something a user has done—for example, a cursor that changes from an arrow to a hand when it rolls over an interactive element during a web visit. This is called a state change in the design biz because it represents a change of state or being. The tech slang for a cursor resting on an interactive element is mouseover.

▶ **Responsive mechanisms:** Something that represents a genuine "receipt" following a conscious action on the part of the user. For example, this might include when the screen goes blank prior to loading a new page, or an onscreen message that tells you a file is downloading or that downloading is complete.

In this section, I focus on transitional and responsive techniques because invitational tricks (blinking, spinning logos, and so on) are more about creating attention than delivering a communicative receipt. Important as these invitational tricks are, they aren't really "feedback" but are "stimuli."

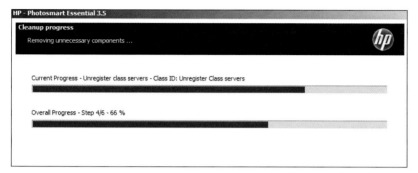

This download box has divided the download/installation process into six steps. The two bars give you good feedback as to how far you are in both the individual steps and the total process. If the download box also indicated how long it takes to complete the task, I'd change the interface rating from "good" to "brilliant."

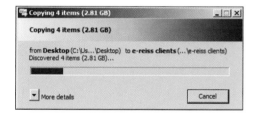

When transferring files from one folder to another, Windows 7 uses this basic bar to show that progress is being made. Both Apple and Android products use similar feedback mechanisms.

A fourth view: "Responsive design"

In the not-so-olden days, if a website had a moderately fluid layout that permitted users to resize a window without destroying a layout, designers were pretty pleased with themselves. But quite recently, designers discovered that what works on a big computer screen may not work as well on a smaller screen on a tablet, smartphone, or car dashboard—and navigational needs may change, too. For example, navigating a smart TV can be something of a challenge if no mouse or trackpad is available; moving a cursor using only an arrow keys is really quite difficult.

Today, with so many different devices on the market it is impossible to design a dedicated interface for them all. Instead, the focus is on responsive designs, which automatically adjust information presentation depending on the type of device on which the information will be displayed. The request could be expanding or contracting the layout to fit the screen or browser window or even changing the layout dramatically or omitting elements. More importantly, the information itself is now being "designed" (written, prioritized, formatted, created, etc.) so that it works well in a variety of display environments. This, not surprisingly, is called responsive content, and it's certainly something we'll all think about for many years to come.

An example of responsive content is eliminating text references to other elements that may might or might not be present on the screen. So, unlike a traditional newspaper article that might refer readers to "the graph on the right," the text is written so that the physical placement (or even presence) of this associated graphic is irrelevant. In short, the creation of responsive content and responsive designs depends on our ability to resize, reposition, cut back, or eliminate elements that are inappropriate to the specific device or screen size.

When testing online products, it's certainly important to change the size of the basic browser window to see if things continue to display properly. But today, you must also check things on tablet computers and smartphones. If the page isn't "responsive" it might be a good idea to make it so, although this is easier said than done, and the technical skills involved are way beyond the scope of this book. What is important, though, is not to let a designer present you or your team with only pretty paper screen mock-ups glued on expensive black cardboard. Press the designer to explain how he or she has built responsiveness into the design templates.

On a related note, from a content point of view, it is generally easier to create a good user experience by scaling up content items created for a smaller screen than to edit down from elements created for full-scale viewing.

Responsive design means that layout and content adjust to fit the medium. This is *The New York Times* website as seen on a PC.

Here is the iPad-friendly application for *The New York Times*.

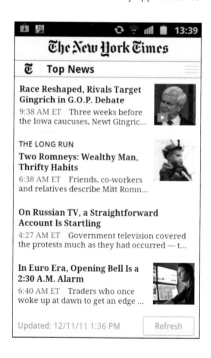

On my Android device, *The New York Times* app is a bare-bones news reader.

"Wake up, you stupid machine!"

Incredibly, a complete lack of feedback is a common usability problem. In the offline world, for example, you expect the cashier at your local supermarket to say "Thank you. Have a nice day." or some other worn-out cliché. Even if the sentiment is tired, to ignore you is simply rude. No matter how banal the response, you still appreciate it. Yet consider your recent online experiences for a moment. How often have you clicked something without knowing whether the machine/server/strange-mechanism-in-cyberspace has actually gotten your message? Pretty often, right? A simple electronic "Have a nice day" might be appreciated.

Earlier today, I noticed that my new laptop was displaying a red X in the status line at the bottom of my desktop screen. I clicked the X and was promptly told I needed to install an updated USB-something-or-other. So I clicked several times more on both the response options, Save and Open. But I received absolutely *no* response from the machine.

The question is, did my click(s) solve my laptop's perceived problem or was something still amiss? How on earth do I know? Because I didn't experience a problem to begin with, I wouldn't even know how to check this.

Follow up: Apparently something happened. Some hours later, my laptop asked "Did this solve your problem?" Alas, the survey didn't let me answer: "I didn't have a problem before you started pestering me." The "Tales from the Trenches" story at the end of this chapter is another example of what happens when no feedback is provided.

The lesson here is this: If you ask someone to do something—and they do it—give them some sign of acknowledgement.

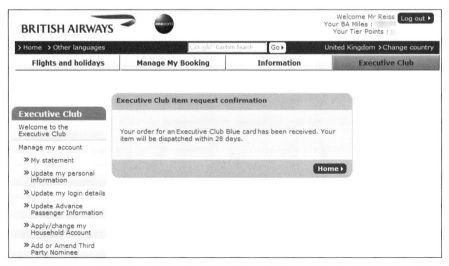

The British Airways' website winged its way out of usability purgatory to become one of the best airline websites around. It's responsive, accurate, and easy-to-use—until you need to order a physical replacement frequent-flyer card. The offline reality doesn't always live up to the online image of service efficiency.

FUD: Fear, uncertainty, doubt

Remember back in the introduction when I mentioned Steve Krug's book, *Don't Make Me Think*? Well, FUD is part of what *makes* people think—but in a negative, worrisome way. Anything you can do to reduce these three issues also improves usability.

▶ **Fear** means that people are scared that something they do will break the system or at least set something unintended in motion that cannot be undone. For example, what happens when you submit information? Did you buy something or merely acknowledge the correctness of something on a form?

▶ **Uncertainty** is related to fear, but in this case, you're not necessarily scared that you'll make a catastrophic decision. You're merely concerned you'll make a wrong decision because your choices are ambiguously presented.[1]

▶ **Doubt** results when people are thinking like mad and come to the conclusion that whatever they do will not lead to a successful conclusion. For example, when *none* of the choices actually makes sense within the context of whatever task the user is trying to accomplish.

The receipts, acknowledgements, response mechanisms—however you choose to identify them—alleviate at least some of the FUD issues, even if they don't necessarily solve a problem. If any kind of responsive action helps you reduce the effects of FUD, you have achieved a major usability victory! In the case of the poor menu choices from the computer store, perhaps some additional text could help. If you put this additional text in one of those little yellow pop-up windows (called an alt attribute), it is a response mechanism. However, creating more descriptive labels might be a better choice so folks don't have to resort to mouseploration to get the cognitive clues they need. Information architects call this "improving the scent" of a label—and although this has more to do with understandability than responsiveness, the two issues are absolutely related, which is why I bring it up now. Mouseploration is discussed later in this chapter in the "A Closer Look at Transitional Techniques" section.

[1] For example, you often see odd menu choices, such as the following that I found on the site for a computer retailer:

▶ Home
▶ Office
▶ High Performance
▶ Extreme Portability

If you want a good laptop for business use and you travel a lot, where would you click? If this was a multiple choice test, I'd want to answer "All of the above."

Search Mail   Search the Web   Show search options
Create a filter

Your message has been sent. View message

com/Banking - Barclay's range of competitive Int. Bank Accounts. Min. £5k d

□   Move to ▼   Labels ▼   More ▼   C

Package - Hi Eric, Did you have the chance to review the document I sent

FatDUX Blog - Eric, it will be difficult to get them all in one call, since they

Another dark pattern? - Hi Harry, Go and blog this! It's really curious stuff -

"Your message has been sent." How nice. How satisfying. How reassuring. Not a shred of FUD here.

f your car doesn't have a central locking systen
loor with your key and then chek the handle to
s a central locking system, often triggered fron
vill probably make a "chirping" sound when it
receipt."

Even though I've been a professional writer most of my life, I still make spelling errors. Microsoft Word underlines my typos and bad spelling with a red line. If it questions my grammar, it underlines in green. Very helpful, responsive feedback.

The laptop choices from HP are typical of the rather ambiguous navigational options available on computer sites. Fear, uncertainty, doubt—where should I click for the powerhouse, lightweight business computer I'm looking for?

A closer look at transitional techniques

The response when your cursor rolls over something on the screen—on mouseover—is incredibly important. Usually, this means the pointer arrow turns into a hand with a pointing finger, which symbolizes that you can click something. In most circumstances, there is no delay whatsoever from one cursor icon to the other.

The main usability problem is not so much the cursor itself as it is the basic visual signal being provided by the web page. For example, one of the most popular blogging tools these days is Word-Press. However, headlines and other clickable items look pretty much like all the other text on the screen—until your cursor arrives. This reduces people on blogs and other sites to scanning a badly designed page using their cursor in order to uncover the clickable items, which are not sending out a strong cognitive signal to show they are, indeed, interactive elements. My personal slang for this curious sweeping back and forth with the mouse cursor looking for links is *mouseploration*.

Of course, with the advent of touchscreen tablet computers and smartphones, mouseploration isn't possible—although the newest generation of screen technology can actually sense the presence of a finger, even if you don't actually tap the screen. In other words, an important responsive element is missing from most touchscreen devices, so you need to send out visible signals in some other way. The second part of this book has an entire chapter devoted to visibility.

For now, keep in mind that whatever you are designing or evaluating must provide immediate transitional responses during use. For example, if a cursor does not change its shape when appropriate, you have a problem that you should correct immediately. And consider having links highlight themselves, change color, or underline themselves on mouseover. Believe me, users will genuinely appreciate this!

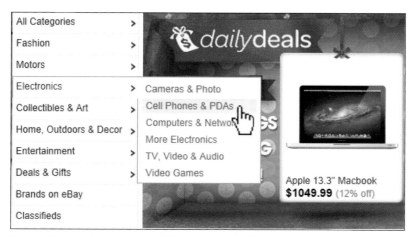

Here, eBay has clearly indicated the relevant top-level category and has highlighted the label of the subcategory I am about to click in the fly-out menu.

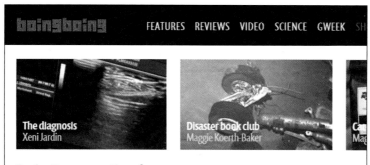

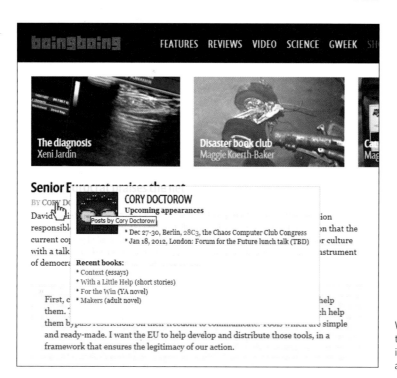

Cory Doctorow's Boing Boing is one of the most popular blogs on the Internet. But much of the interactivity is not immediately visible. Although there is a red link in the first paragraph, most users won't realize that the headline and several other items are also interactive.

When mousing over Cory's name, the reader gets both a pop-up information box and a little yellow alt attribute text box.

Transitional techniques and physical objects

On/off knobs that click. Physical keyboards that provide tactile resistance. Touchscreen keyboards that vibrate when touched. All these techniques provide here-and-now feedback that is incredibly useful when you operate physical devices.

One of the challenges facing the people working with virtual reality is that apart from visual and audio signals, there isn't much in terms of other sensory feedback. Even though we might be able to "virtually" pick up stuff, we cannot yet feel it. It's like trying to catch a wisp of smoke in your hand; there is no substance. Until we can re-create the tactile feedback associated with "substance," virtual reality is going to remain much more *virtual* than *real*.

Think about how you can improve the transitional feedback mechanisms of any physical affordances on your stuff—knobs, dials, levers, switches, buttons, keys, handles, and so on. These "clicks" are important, too.

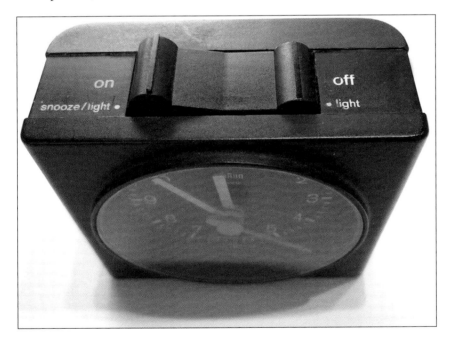

I love this alarm clock from Braun. The controls on the top make it easy to turn the alarm on and off. And because the control rocks back and forth, I can easily see if I've remembered to set the alarm. There's lots of good cognitive feedback in a highly functional design.

Response mechanisms in the online environment

We are always reassured when our machine tells us that it is thinking. In 1983, when I saw the first Apple Lisa, the precursor to the Macintosh, I loved the little hourglass icon that basically told me: "Hi, Eric. I got your message and I'm doing what you asked me to do. This is going to take a little time, so be patient. As long as you see this cute animated icon, you'll know I'm busy trying to complete the task you assigned me."

Quite a lot of information packed into a little onscreen symbol. Along with the Back button and the Undo command, I think this is one of the coolest things ever to come along.

There are countless other versions of this type of feedback—from counting hands and running dogs to wristwatches and the infamous Apple "spinning wait cursor," which, due to slow functional responsiveness, has acquired a number of not-so-friendly nicknames, such as "spinning beach ball from Hell." The lesson here is that providing feedback in itself often alleviates a problem, but it doesn't always solve one. For this reason, graphic techniques that also show that progress is being made are sometimes even better options when lengthy operations are involved.

In addition to basic onscreen messages, such as, "Your file was successfully downloaded," and various animated widgets, there are a variety of design patterns that are now associated with the completion of various tasks. Here are a few of the more popular conventions:

▶ **Brighten and dim:** Brightening a specific area to show that it is now active, or dimming part of a screen until an operation is completed.

▶ **Zoom:** Zooming in while a particular process in underway, or zooming out (or collapsing a window) when a process is completed.

▶ **Sounds:** Distinctive melodies or noises that are associated with specific actions. We are probably most familiar with those on our mobile phones that tell us that mail or an SMS has arrived.

There are literally thousands of other techniques, some good, some bad. But whatever response mechanisms you decide to use, if the user can see, hear, or feel them—and understands their meaning—you're going to be in good shape usability-wise.

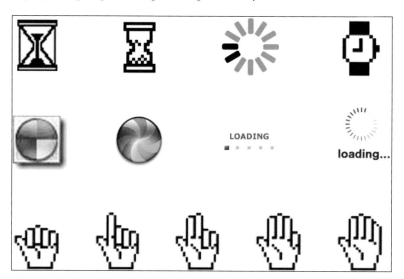

The hourglass wait-icon debuted on the original Apple Lisa in 1983 still ranks as one of the most original feedback mechanisms I've ever seen. It's since been used in various forms by both Apple and Microsoft. The signal it sends is valuable: "I'm working on your stuff. Take a break. I'll solve this problem."

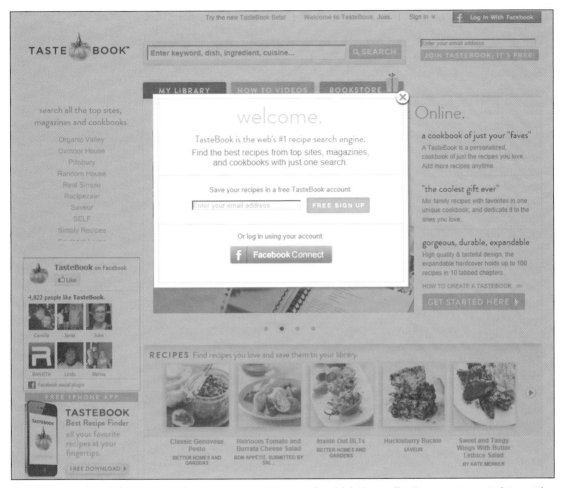

Dimming a portion of the screen makes it easy to spot the area in which the application expects me to interact in some way. Brightening a portion of a screen can have a similar effect.

Response mechanisms in physical objects

Like their onscreen counterparts, physical response mechanisms provide valuable cognitive feedback that something is happening or has been accomplished. Let's take a moment to think about locking things, such as cars and houses.

If your car doesn't have a central locking system, the chances are you lock the car door with your key and then check the handle to make sure it is locked. If there is a central locking system, often triggered from a button on the key itself, the car probably makes a chirping sound when it is locked, thus providing the needed receipt. Hearing the ka-chunk of the locks is also reassuring.

The majority of people also check the door of their house when they leave by giving it an extra tug to make sure it is really locked. That's because most locks don't really provide very good feedback. Perhaps house doors should chirp and ka-chunk, too.

The lesson, though, is that as in every conversational interaction, response mechanisms that provide sensory feedback help smooth things along and eliminate FUD.

This classic counter provides good tactile feedback and an audible click each time the button is depressed. In other words, you never need to look at the counter while you're actually doing the counting.

OOPS! I JUST ORDERED THREE ROLLS-ROYCES
A TALE FROM THE TRENCHES

DURING THE EARLY YEARS of the web, the concept of a "shopping basket" or "shopping cart" was still considered an analogy rather than a metaphor.

Just for the record, an analogy is "this [thing] *is like* [another thing]. Example, "My computer *is like* a filing cabinet." "Filing cabinet" is the analogy.

A metaphor is "this [thing] *is* [another thing]. Example, "This chip is my computer's memory." "Memory" is the metaphor.

So, with the semantic lecture out of the way, let me tell you a story.

One afternoon, back around 1997, a colleague of mine told me that a famous London automobile dealer was now selling Rolls-Royces online. I was given this piece of information for two reasons: I was fascinated with e-commerce, and I had a weakness for English cars, which (expensively) continues to this day.

Naturally, I immediately visited the site.[2]

The site was filled with luscious photos of Jaguars, Astons, and Rolls-Royces. Somewhat incongruously, there was a "shopping basket" icon at the top of the page. Keep in mind that in 1997 the idea of a "shopping basket" was still more analogy than a metaphor. Anyway, it was almost impossible *not* to visualize (or at least laugh at the thought of) a pristinely polished luxury car pulled off the shelf and dumped into a nondescript wire container on wheels.

Evil man that I am, this was *precisely* what I did.

But the page didn't respond. So I clicked again. And again.

Server response times were agonizingly slow back then, so I was used to waiting. Today, we are less patient, which exacerbates this particular problem.

[2] Alas, in writing this so many years later, I have no screen-shots to illustrate the story. And although I remember the dealership, it would be totally unfair to single them out for bad design decisions that are now ancient history—at least when measured in Internet years (which by my own estimate equal about 4.7 calendar years if you compare off- and online business cycles).

MORE >

▶ **OOPS! I JUST ORDERED THREE ROLLS-ROYCES**
A TALE FROM THE TRENCHES

While I was waiting, the phone rang. I chatted a bit. Afterward, I went over to our company canteen to get a cup of coffee. When I returned to my desk, I discovered that whatever this automobile website had been doing was now completed and I had been sent on to the payment page. In the meantime, it seems that each time I had impatiently clicked, I had added a new Rolls-Royce to my basket. I had ordered three in all. And in the same color—how boring.

So, with three expensive cars in my basket, and a check-out system that was giving me grief (but surprisingly *not* for exceeding my credit limit), my solution was simply to turn off my computer and go home for the day. I often wonder what the outcome would have been if I had accidentally succeeded in buying a car or two—at least in cyberspace. But that's what comes when you design an unresponsive system. Of course, my wife would quickly respond to tell me we already have a perfectly good car, which is another story entirely.

TEN RESPONSE MECHANISMS TO CONSIDER

1. When a button is clicked, can you see that it "reacts"?

2. When a file has been saved, can you see that it has been saved?

3. If your cursor rolls over a link or other interactive object, does the cursor change shape to indicate that something is clickable?

4. Can your site be resized on a computer screen? What happens when you look at it on a tablet or smartphone? Will it work on a smart TV?

5. Try to complete some basic tasks, such as downloading a file or clicking through a check-out procedure. Are there any times when you wish the site had acknowledged some action on your part?

6. Are all lengthy procedures, such as downloading a file, providing ongoing feedback regarding the progress that has been made?

7. If you are dealing with a physical object, is it providing feedback? Do you know when something has been switched on or off? Or turned up or turned down?

8. Is any feedback you receive arriving in a timely manner? Or are you first getting messages long after an action has been undertaken?

9. Are the response mechanisms understandable? Or are icons and other signals forcing users to guess? Are you applying established best practices or are you inventing them from scratch? Would your next-door neighbor understand them? Or your family?

10. Does the layout and quality of the content reflect the limitations of the particular device on which it is viewed? If the content is different from one device to another, has it been scaled up or cut down to fit appropriately? Scaling up is generally the better choice.

OTHER BOOKS
YOU MIGHT LIKE

As you may have guessed by now, the books I recommend are not always 100 percent focused on the subject of the specific chapter. But they are all highly relevant within the context of the chapter in which they are presented, contain vital information, and are well-written.

▶ *Designing Web Interfaces*, Bill Scott and Theresa Neil, O'Reilly, 2009

▶ *Neuro Web Design*, Susan Weinschenk, New Riders, 2009

▶ *Responsive Web Design*, Ethan Marcotte, A Book Apart, 2011

THINGS TO
GOOGLE

▶ Responsive content

▶ Responsive web design

▶ Navigation feedback

Chapter Three

Ergonomic

Ergonomics, also called human factors, is the study of how devices can be designed so they match both our physical and psychological abilities. For the most part, people first meet the term when discussing workplace ergonomics—office chair adjustment, desk height, the position of a computer screen, and so on. But the principles of ergonomics apply as much to what happens on a screen as to things going on around it.

Online design meets offline ergonomics: When I print electronic boarding passes, I fold them and put them in my jacket pocket. The British Airways version features a bar code along the top edge, which is easy to scan both at security and at the gate. The SAS version features a wide top margin and a bar code running down the side. I have to unfold it to have it scanned, and often the part of the code in the crease has worn off. Some airlines actually put the code at the bottom of the page, which is completely idiotic.

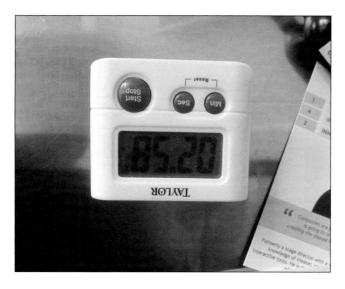

The magnet on this refrigerator timer is not strong enough to keep the unit upright. A functional problem or an ergonomic problem? I'd say both (being forced to read stuff upside down is clearly related to ergonomics, right?). The magnet was such a simple, obvious feature that the designers clearly forgot to test it on a metal surface.

Henry Dreyfuss: Introducing ergonomics to industrial design

Although the American industrial designer, Henry Dreyfuss didn't invent the subject of ergonomics,[1] he did get it out of the universities and into the world of design. His semi-autobiographical work, *Designing for People* (Simon & Schuster, 1955) remains an industry classic.

Dreyfuss' key contribution was his two human models Joe and Josephine, who represent typical male and female measurement sets for mid-twentieth century North Americans. Although many design philosophies have changed over the past 60 years, an amazing number of physical objects are still built based on Dreyfuss' anthropometric data.

Here are 12 basic principles of ergonomics[2]:

1. Work in neutral postures.
2. Reduce excessive force.
3. Keep everything in easy reach.
4. Work at proper heights.
5. Reduce excessive motions.
6. Minimize fatigue and static load.
7. Minimize pressure points.
8. Provide clearance.
9. Move, exercise, and stretch.
10. Maintain a comfortable environment.
11. Enhance clarity and understanding.
12. Improve work organization.

---

[1] That honor goes to the ancient Greeks; the actual term "ergonomic" was coined by a Pole, Wojciech Jastrzebowski, back in in 1857.

[2] If you Google "ergonomics" you'll find many similar lists, some with more points, some with fewer and with a variety of wordings. I'm not entirely sure that an "official" list exists. This is my own best shot, combining the best from several lists I've found.

What makes these principles important to us in terms of usability is that even though they are based on actions and effects in the physical world, they also have a huge effect on onscreen design. For example, the cursor acts as our electronic finger. Just like a real finger, there are certain movements it can and cannot make. Moreover, with the advent of touchscreens, our fingers often *are* cursors, and suddenly we find ourselves wrestling with online and offline ergonomics simultaneously.

If you are designing physical stuff, you are probably already familiar with these principles, so I'm not going to get into a detailed discussion of industrial design. However, for those of you working with interactive media, I'm going to share some of my thoughts on how ergonomics relate to evaluating and improving the onscreen experience.

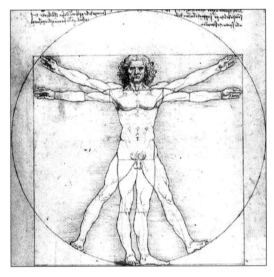

Leonardo illustrated the concept. . . .

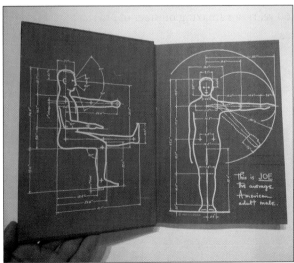

. . . but Henry put in the measurements. (Photo of end-pages of first edition of Henry Dreyfuss' 1955 classic, *Designing for People*.)

The flask on the left was designed by the renowned Danish architect Erik Magnussen. He eliminated sharp edges and protrusions that could catch the flask in a pocket. Alas, the cap is impossible to grasp and the flask can't be placed upright on a table. Oops. The version at the right is cheap, but far better from an ergonomic point-of-view.

When the power goes out in a hurricane, flashlights can provide ambient light when placed in the middle of a table, but only if they have a flat base. This one helped my Florida family weather hurricanes Francis, Ivan, Katrina, Rita, and Wilma.

Buttons: Why bigger sometimes *is* better

Students of Human-Computer Interaction (HCI) will tell you about Fitts' Law:

$$MT = a + b \log_2(2A/W + c)$$

This rather sophisticated mathematical equation predicts that the time required to rapidly move to a target area is a function of the distance to the target and the size of the target. Pretty straightforward, huh?

Actually it *is* simple—a big button is faster to locate and click than a little button.

This is a critical concept when talking about onscreen ergonomics. It relates directly to two of the principles I just listed: "keep everything in easy reach" and "enhance clarity and understanding."

In practice, bigger clickable links make life easier for the user. One of the current issues in usability is the convention of the <u>embedded hyperlink</u>. On a big screen, these are generally pretty easy to use. But what about using big fingers on a small touchscreen device? If you haven't tried this, the next time you pass an Apple Store, go in and play with an iPad. Fingers are not always ideal for navigating a traditional website on a tablet—and they're even less agile when navigating on a smartphone.

Today, we're seeing the advent of smart TVs—browser-enabled interactive televisions that can access content from the Internet and stream on-demand programming, thus reducing the dependence on traditional broadcast offerings.

Right now, there are no real standards for the controllers that help you move the cursor around the screen. There are PC-like trackpads, traditional arrow keys, and infrared pointers. You can even link some devices, such as your smartphone or tablet, and use them as controllers, But the truth is, it's just plain difficult to hit little buttons on a screen located on the other side of the room. My own rule of thumb (or index finger) is this: If you can't easily poke something on a smartphone, you're going to have problems navigating the same website or app on a smart TV. Please consider that even a huge TV often represents a very small part of the viewer's total field-of-view and is frequently smaller than that of a smartphone held in the hand.

As I suggested in Chapter Two, responsive design is playing a huge role in the development of future interactive products. Keep this in mind. Also remember that although you personally might not like or use alternative interfaces, there is no guarantee that others share your views.

In a nutshell, keep your buttons big and easy to access across all platforms.

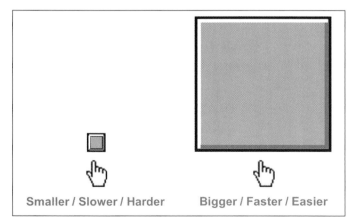

Smaller / Slower / Harder   Bigger / Faster / Easier

Bigger targets are quicker to acquire and use than smaller targets. This is an important concept if you are designing missile systems for the military. But it's just as important for those of us working with interactive media—bigger buttons are generally better.

The latest version of the iPod shuffle® is so small that it is almost impossible to clip it to clothing without also pushing the control buttons. The earlier, longer version of this product took this into consideration. An ergonomic lesson learned—and then forgotten.

Milliseconds count

A lot of sites these days think that "keeping everything in easy reach" means nesting navigation menus so visitors can get to something deep within the site without clicking on any other pages. As a result, you find a lot of drop-down menus that then trigger a secondary menu that "flies out" from the side.

Well, let me be blunt: This technique may be useful, but there's a long road from useful to usable. Try navigating one of these with your finger or a TV controller and you'll quickly curse the designer. And even with a mouse, it can be tricky to grab the word or phrase on which you want to click. That said, there are a couple of very basic things you can do that will dramatically improve usability.

Make sure that the clickable area is larger than just the words in the link. You really don't want to make these active areas too small.

Make sure you give people enough time to maneuver the cursor into position. Although I hate to get into technical nitty-gritty, the timing issue is really quite important, so let me share some of the current best practices:

▶ Let the cursor "hover" over a link for about half a second before triggering any menu expansion. This helps avoid the "blooming flower" problem I encountered with the Interflora site (see "Tales from the Trenches" at the end of this chapter).

▶ After an animated menu has been triggered, it should display as quickly as possible—in less than 1/10 second if possible.

▶ When the visitor moves the cursor away from the menu, wait half a second before you collapse the menu. This gives people a chance to move the cursor more sloppily as they navigate and cut corners, thus reducing the need to stay strictly within the active areas of the menu

▶ That said, when the menu *does* collapse, it should do so as quickly as it appeared.

From a functionality point-of-view, make sure to check the timing of these actions on a slow device and not just on your own faster-than-lightning computer. In general, you should also be checking your overall server response times on a dial-up connection and not just on broadband. You'd be surprised at how many people don't have any access to broadband, particularly in rural areas. And if you are working in an international environment, keep in mind that outside North America, Europe, and a few countries along the Pacific rim, there are many regions that still have no broadband access at all, but merely slow dial-up and mobile connections.

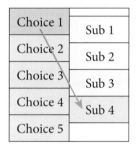

By delaying the collapse of a drop-down/fly-out menu, visitors can move the cursor directly on the diagonal without triggering other menu items or losing the one they wanted to click.

Bring on the scientists

The academic community is doing a lot of research in the area of onscreen ergonomics. And some of the discoveries are quite eye-opening—literally. New eyetracking studies (recording where people look while viewing a website) demonstrate that people read very differently on a screen. Rather than starting at the top and reading all the way through in a linear fashion, people tend to quickly scan a page looking for a word that triggers their attention. They then skim the text, looking for more cognitive triggers. Only then do most people start to read in detail.

I'll bet that when you first opened this book, you flipped through quickly, read the captions next to a few pictures that caught your eye, and then perhaps looked at a paragraph of text on the same page or the facing page. No, I'm not a mind-reader, this is merely a fairly well-established pattern.

"First word after the bullet"

One of the most important findings related to onscreen ergonomics relates to how best to create long lists of links. Usability expert Jakob Nielsen talks about the "F-pattern."[3] Basically, what happens is that when people skim a list, they look at the first word after the bullet symbol. Occasionally, this word entices them to read the entire link.

The result is that when you look at an eyetracking map—usually a so-called "heat map" where the areas looked at get more red the more a person stared at them—you see a kind of F-shaped pattern emerge. Users scan the first words, skim a few links, actually read a couple in detail. Let me give you an example:

Which of these two lists is easier for you to scan?

List One:

▶ Subregional office for Central Africa

▶ Subregional office for East Africa

▶ Subregional office for West Africa

▶ Subregional office for North Africa

▶ Subregional office for Southern Africa

▶ Subregional office for Sahil Region

List Two:

▶ Central Africa - subregional office

▶ East Africa - subregional office

▶ West Africa - subregional office

▶ North Africa - subregional office

▶ Southern Africa - subregional office

▶ Sahil Region - subregional office

The first list is taken from the old website for the International Labour Organisation in Geneva. Happily, the website underwent a major redesign in 2010.

What this means is that when you prepare lists—lists of links in particular—you want to make sure the most important words are right at the beginning, not at the end. This also applies to the machine-readable meta-title that announces the name of a specific web page in a list of search results. So look critically at any lists, menus, or links that don't begin with the most important words and keep in mind that your company name is probably *not* the most important information in the list.

---

[3]For some really good online resources, check out www.useit.com/eyetracking.

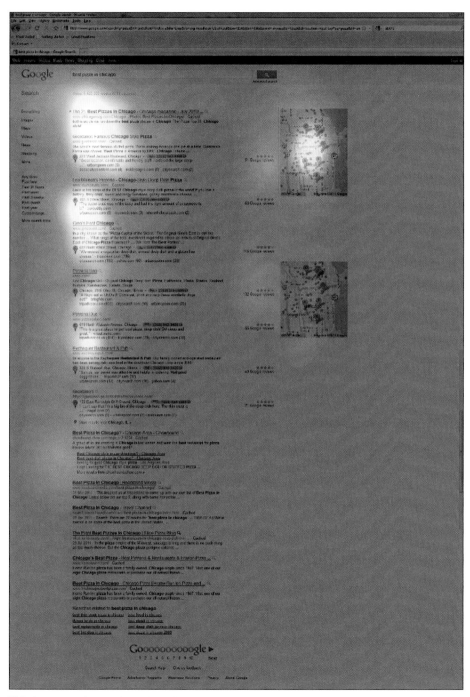

This heat map clearly shows how the eye scans a page of links. When creating lists or headlines, make sure to put the important words up front. (Image courtesy of Dr. Peter J. Meyers and SEOmoz.)

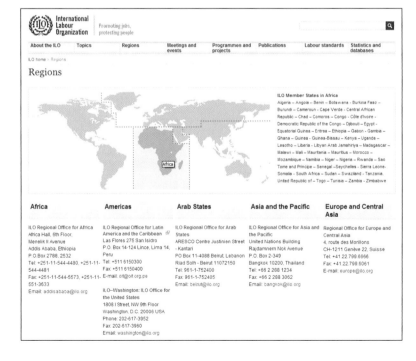

Regions and Technical Cooperation (REGIONS)

> Development Cooperation (CODEV)
>> Universitas: Innovation, education and training for Decent Work and Human Development
>
> Field Programmes in Africa (AFRICA)
>> Regional Office for Africa: Addis Ababa
>> Subregional Office for Central Africa: SRO-Yaoundé
>> Subregional Office for East Africa: SRO-Addis Ababa
>> Subregional Office for West Africa: SRO-Abidjan (temporary location: Dakar)
>> Subregional Office for North Africa: SRO-Cairo
>> Subregional Office for Southern Africa: SRO-Harare
>> Subregional Office for the Sahel Region: SRO-Dakar
>> ILO Office in Algiers: ILO-Algiers
>> ILO Office in Antananarivo: ILO-Antananarivo
>> ILO Office in Dar es Salaam: ILO-Dar es salaam
>> ILO Office in Kinshasa: ILO-Kinshasa
>> ILO Office in Lagos: ILO-Lagos
>> ILO Office in Lusaka: ILO-Lusaka
>> ILO Office in Pretoria: ILO-Pretoria
>
> Field Programmes in Latin America and the Caribbean (AMERICAS)
>> ILO Regional Office for Latin America and the Caribbean (Web site in Spanish)
>> Subregional Office for the Andean Countries: SRO-Lima (Web site in Spanish)
>> Subregional Office for the Caribbean: SRO-Port of Spain
>> Subregional Office for the South Cone of Latin America: SRO-Santiago (Web site in Spanish)
>> Subregional Office for Central America: ILO-San José
>> ILO Office for Mexico and Cuba: ILO-Mexico (Web site in Spanish)
>> ILO Office in Argentina: ILO-Buenos Aires (Web site in Spanish)
>> ILO Office in Brazil: ILO-Brasilia (Web site in Portuguese)
>> The Inter-American Centre for Knowledge Development in Vocational Training (CINTERFOR)
>

This portion of the original list of regional offices for the International Labour Organisation was incredibly difficult to scan.

The redesigned ILO site makes it easy to locate offices thanks to a cleaner design and more ergonomic navigation.

Tabs and other keyboard shortcuts

Back in the early days of personal computing, Bill Gates came up with a great operating system. He called it the Disk Operating System. We call it DOS. It made Bill a zillionaire and Microsoft a world leader in software.

Mind you, this was all in the days before Apple got us hooked on the graphic user interface (GUI) and using a mouse to point at things on the screen.[4] Instead, DOS users hit the Tab key to move from one menu choice to the next, or from one form field to the next. And this convention has stuck.

Despite the advent of the mouse, a lot of users don't want to take their hands off the keyboard to do something. They still want to be able to tab their way from one field to the next when booking a hotel room or use a simple keyboard shortcut to save a document on which they're working. Here's an example.

The bookkeeper at my company reluctantly surrendered her DOS accounting program because it simply would not work with her fast, new computer. Her work routine was fairly typical: Use the right hand to type in numbers from the numeric keypad; use the left hand to tab to the appropriate entry field. This absolutely served to reduce excessive motions. (Remember the ergonomics' principles at the beginning of this chapter?) It also helped maintain a comfortable environment, minimized fatigue, and kept everything within easy reach.

We evaluated several new bookkeeping programs. The one we chose was the *only* one that provided decent keyboard-based alternatives to mouse movements. Suddenly, usability ergonomics play into the business case, so if you have an application of some kind, particularly one that involves repetitive tasks, such as entering data for hundreds of similar items (receipts, for example), this could be an incredibly important issue on which to focus.

But keyboard shortcuts provide more than just convenience. For example, Repetitive Strain Injury (RSI)—also known as carpal tunnel syndrome—can also be reduced through keyboard shortcuts. Not only is constant usage of a mouse potentially harmful, but if someone already has a serious injury, keyboard shortcuts make it much easier to adopt voice-recognition tools, thus eliminating the need to touch the keyboard or mouse at all.

If you want to experiment with the idea of tabbing and keyboard shortcuts online, visit any airline or hotel website and make a booking (no, you don't actually have to buy anything—just play with the booking engine). Some sites let you tab in your travel dates, others make you click on a calendar. Ideally, both options should be available.

[4]The computer mouse was invented in the 1960s by Doug Engelbart at the Augmentation Research Center. But Apple gave it a permanent place on the desktop.

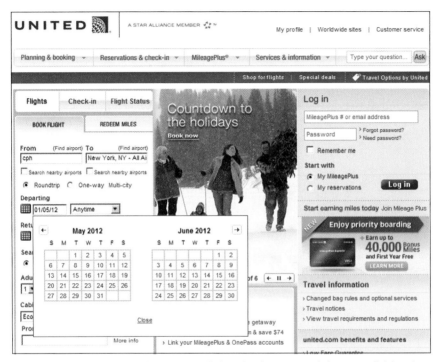

The United Airlines website is pretty good about letting users tab from one field to the next—until the time comes to enter a date. Alas, I couldn't manage to do this without using the mouse. But I shouldn't pick on United; most airline and hotel sites feature the same unnecessary problem.

Provide clearance

As a basic ergonomic principle, to provide clearance means making sure two shopping carts can pass each other in the supermarket aisle. Or that tall people don't hit their heads on the doorframe. Or that buttons are big enough to punch comfortably . . . er . . . we already talked about that.

Online, many sites these days now include little animated boxes and widgets that provide extra navigational options, special information, or access to extra functions. These tend to pop up on mouseover, although some just float around on the edges of a page. The problem is that sometimes they won't go away, thus obscuring other pieces of information.

If you're working with an overly enthusiastic design and development team, it's sometimes easy to forget the ergonomic basics as cool tools are introduced to the layout. Well, now you know—so watch out that you don't do more harm than good to your product!

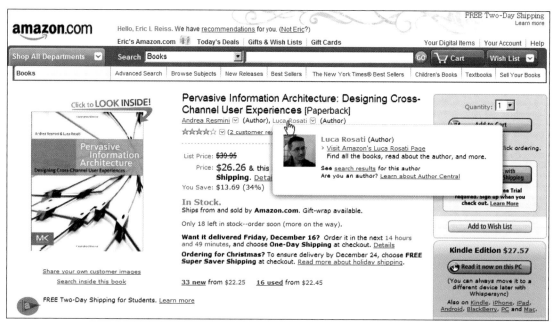

Amazon has lots of useful pop-ups, such as this author information box. They generally work quite well and go away again as appropriate. That's particularly good in this case where the box partially obscures the shopping-cart button.

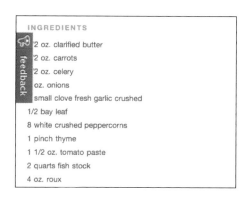

The iPad version of the Tastebook.com site has an irritating floating widget on the left-hand side that effectively obscures the measurement data on most of the recipes.

"Go to the back of the line"

How often has a website discarded information that you carefully entered into a form? Probably more than once. It usually happens when you submit a form and the computer or website perceives a problem of some kind. If the form is forgiving, it will tell you where you made the error and retain all of the information that it is willing to accept.

But if your form is grouchy—as many are—it will tell you to click the Back button and correct your error. And in clicking the Back button, you might be horrified to discover that the application threw out *everything* you previously typed in, making you start all over again.

This is as frustrating as it is unnecessary. If this is a problem on your site, fix it—I know of no faster way to annoy customers than to make them submit the same information again and again because a form (and the related business rules) are badly designed.

Improve work organization

In the physical world, the improve-work-organization ergonomic principle means making sure that there is a sensible task flow—printer paper is next to the printer; products move sensibly from one station to the next along an assembly line; after a process is started, it is not interrupted.

Well, in the online world, many sites and apps have not yet embraced the principle. As usual, forms are a major culprit. The problem occurs when someone starts filling out a multi-part form and halfway through the third screen, he or she discovers that the form wants information that is not immediately available. Allowing the user can save his or her work and return at some later time is a reasonable option. Ideally, people would know exactly what is going to be needed *before* they start a process—much like listing all the ingredients at the top of a recipe.

Let me give you a classic example of how *not* to do things.

Eric and the IRS

The United States Internal Revenue Service (IRS)—the tax department—requires an Employee Identification Number if you want to transport goods out of the United States. When my mom passed away, I needed to close up her house in Miami, FL and get some books, furniture, and personal papers to my home in Copenhagen. So I needed an EIN number. Oh boy. . . .

The online IRS experience starts with a dire warning that if I don't complete my form in 15 minutes it will time out and that I cannot save an incomplete form. Sadly, there was no indication of what I would need, so it was difficult to prepare for what might come. I thought I'd play it safe and gather *everything* I knew about the estate. I cautiously clicked APPLY ONLINE NOW.

Amazingly, the form was not available in Denmark on a Sunday as the digital "online assistant" apparently only works during normal business hours in the U.S. (Eastern time)! But when I finally got into the system, I made it through several screens before I got stuck—the form wanted the date the estate was created, funded, or probated. Oops. . . .

Anyway, I got timed out, tried again, ran into another issue, timed out, tried a third time, timed out, and finally turned this all over to my patient, capable, expensive lawyer. Several hundred dollars in legal fees later, I was all set. Bad form. Bad ergonomics. Bad service. Bad experience. Great example for a book on usability!

PS—I actually tried to game the system at one point to see all of the information they needed by typing in nonsense just to get to the next screen. But alas, no. The application wanted real, sensible data, so I was never able to build the "list of ingredients" I needed. I see this as a clear ergonomic failure that relates directly to work organization.

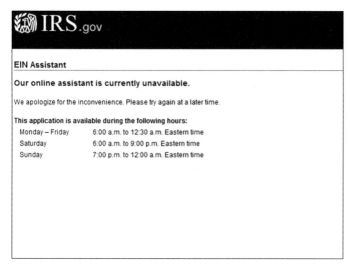

Incredibly, the Internal Revenue Service's online forms have opening hours. I wonder if they also get time off for Christmas and New Year. . . .

No matter how hard I tried, the IRS site kept asking for information that wasn't immediately available. As a result, I was repeatedly timed out and had to start from scratch.

The "silent usher"

I don't know which architect originally came up with this brilliant concept, but I learned about it during a tour of New York's Radio City Music Hall many years ago. At the base of several of the staircases, there are big columns that divide the crowd descending the stairs after a show. Many of them are not actually holding up the roof, but were specifically placed where they are *because* there was a need to do some passive crowd control.

In the online arena, we face similar problems. We have a lot of information that can potentially "descend the stairs" and meet website visitors. If we can eliminate the unnecessary or unwanted information early on, the chances are that what remains will be more relevant. It will also become more visible as there will be fewer distracting elements and links.

I mention this now because I think the concept of the silent usher can certainly be applied to websites, apps, and industrial interfaces. And I hope you will start thinking about it and how it can help you make your stuff even easier to use.

The "silent usher" at New York's Radio City Music Hall helps divide and disperse crowds at the bottom of the stairs. Online, we also want to provide clearly visible devices that help visitors reach their destination without too many detours. (Photo courtesy of Matthew Fetchko)

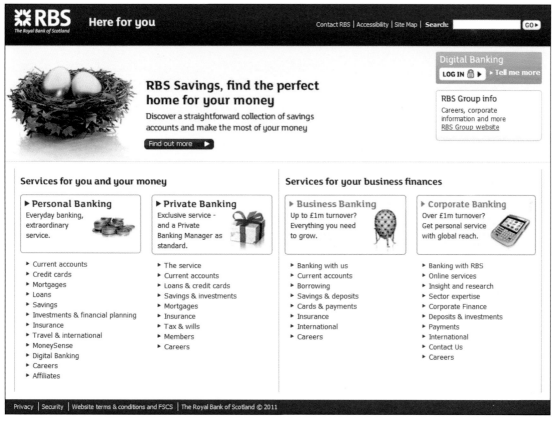

The Royal Bank of Scotland provides a prominent "silent usher" that splits visitors into private and business segments. A further "silent usher" subdivision ensures that people get where they're going faster and with fewer irrelevant onscreen distractions.

▶ **FLOWERS THAT BLOOM ON THE SCREEN**
A TALE FROM THE TRENCHES

A FEW YEARS AGO, I decided I would surprise my wife and send her some flowers at work. A quick search led me to the Danish Interflora site, which featured some lovely animated drop-down menus. When one of the main menu items was rolled over (not clicked), a small flower bloomed as the menu unfolded. It was a lovely, if slightly corny effect.

I managed to get through the ordering process very easily, gave them my credit-card information and everything seemed to be going smoothly. Until. . . .

Following the successful submission of my order, I was asked to print out a page of data that included my order number and some other details that I might want to keep handy. So, I tried to print the page.

At the time, my version of Internet Explorer had a print icon on the left-hand side of the "command" toolbar at the top of the browser window. However, my cursor was in the opposite corner of the page, on the lower right, next to the "downward scroll" icon.

Big deal. How tough could it be to move a cursor from one corner of a window to another to print a page? Tougher than you might think! Here's what happened.

Every time I rolled over the menu bar at the top of the Interflora page, it triggered the blossoming flower and the drop-down menu, which wouldn't close until I rolled over another menu item or clicked on something other than the browser toolbar. As a result, the critical information on the page was hidden from view when I printed the page.

The solution was to sneak the cursor around the edge of the screen and up to the printer icon. I was so amused by this silly problem and awkward solution that I actually captured the entire sequence in a short digital film, which I have since used in lectures around the world. It always gets a good laugh.

And just for the record, the real-world flowers I sent were equally appreciated.

FLOWERS THAT BLOOM ON THE SCREEN
A TALE FROM THE TRENCHES

The Interflora order page, waiting to be printed. All I have to do is move my cursor from the lower-right hand corner to the printer icon at the upper left . . .

. . . but every time I got near the top menu, it bloomed and expanded, covering much of the important order information. This site was active for several years from about 2006. Today, the visual gimmicks have been abandoned and the redesigned site works perfectly.

TEN QUESTIONS TO HELP YOU AVOID ACHES AND PAINS DUE TO BAD ERGONOMICS

1. Are the buttons big enough to click easily with a mouse?
2. Are they still big enough if you need to use your finger on a touchscreen?
3. Are the drop-down menus easy to "catch" with the cursor? Are there timing issues that need to be addressed?
4. Are you providing keyboard shortcuts as alternatives to mouse movements?
5. Can users tab from one form-field to the next?
6. Are elements that must be used simultaneously also visible simultaneously?
7. Do you have elements on the screen that are getting in the way of each other?
8. Can you provide the equivalent of a "silent usher" to help people figure out what to do?
9. Are visual gimmicks making your stuff more difficult to use?
10. Are there any illogical task sequences or workflow interruptions that you can change or avoid to make things easier for the user?

OTHER BOOKS YOU MIGHT LIKE

If you're seriously interested in design, here are a few brilliant books to consider:

- *Designing for People*, Henry Dreyfuss, Simon and Schuster, 1955
- *Human Factors and Web Development*, Julie Ratner, CRC Press, 2002
- *Handbook of Human Factors and Ergonomics*, Gavriel Salvendy, Wiley, 2006

THINGS TO GOOGLE

- Anthropometrics
- "Joe and Josephine"
- Henry Dreyfuss
- Human factors
- Eyetracking
- Heat maps

Chapter Four

Convenient

Convenient is one of those pesky adjectives. According to the dictionary, it can mean a couple of things:

1. Suited to one's comfort or ease

2. Placed near at hand

So far so good. The problem arises when you factor in point-of-view; "convenience" is *always* in the eye of the beholder.

When it comes to usability, what is convenient for a designer, programmer, site owner, service provider, and so on is almost never the same as what is convenient for the user of the stuff in question. Let me give you an example.

A couple of years ago, I attended a meeting in someone's office—a fairly large office as these things go. To get to this room, I passed along a long corridor with doors to other offices on either side. Upon entering any of these spaces, a visitor would find a whiteboard just to the left, on the same wall as the door. The window was on the opposite wall and desks were usually placed near the windows.

What made this tidy (and fairly uniform) arrangement odd was the positioning of the plastic channel containing the power, telephone, and computer cables. Rather than running along the baseboard under the window, next to the desk as would be expected, the channel ran across the tops of all of the door frames.

I was so amazed by this comically useless installation that I took a picture, which I share here. When I asked how such a silly thing could have occurred, I was told, "This was easiest for the electrician." Convenient for him, perhaps, but idiotic from a user's point-of-view (POV).

So, what POV did your design team take when making your stuff convenient? That of a project owner or of a genuine user? That's really one of the key questions you need to ask yourself when evaluating stuff in terms of both usability and usefulness.

In this office, the electrical, network, and telephone cables are all installed in a single, convenient channel—inconveniently located high above the whiteboard! "Convenience" is very much a matter of perspective; are you building stuff or using it?

In this Danish office, the electrical, network, and telephone cables and outlets are all installed in a single, convenient channel—inconveniently located high above the whiteboard! "Convenience" is very much a matter of perspective—are you building stuff or using it?

Giving inconvenience a positive spin

Sometimes, "convenience" is given spin in a vain attempt to make users feel as though poor usability is actually working in their favor. For example, whenever someone tells me, "For your convenience . . .," I know that I'm about to experience something very IN-convenient. Here are a couple of quick stories.

The first is from the men's department at a department store. I had found some slacks I wanted to try on, so I set out in search of a changing room. When I finally found one, it was locked. A sign on the door read: "For your convenience, dressing rooms are located on the other side of this floor." No, if they wanted to provide convenience, they would have unlocked *all* the changing rooms.

The second example is from a major chain hotel in Portland, OR. With an ice-bucket in hand, I wandered through several long corridors until I found a utility room. Here, there was a wonderful sign: "For your convenience, ice machines are located on the floors above and below this floor." Sorry, this spin left me cold (and my drink warm). Basically, the hotel is telling me they've removed about half of their ice machines.

"For your convenience . . ."? As they say back in my home state of Texas, "Don't pee on my boots and tell me it's raining."

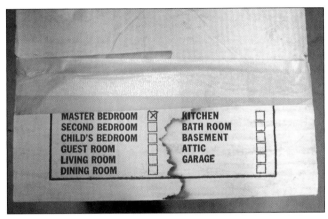

A simple, practical checklist on the side of a moving box. Good usability.

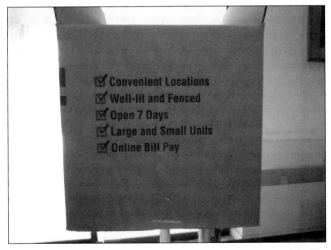

The designers of this moving box decided to waste space with silly advertising instead of useful options. Bad usability. And think, it's just a cardboard box. . . .

Eric's advice for the lovelorn

Permit me yet another short digression. Someone once said (quite wisely) that we *like* someone *because* of their character traits. But we *love* someone *despite* their character traits.

Although convenience is very much in the eye of the beholder, when we *love* something—including websites, apps, and inanimate objects—we tend to be forgiving. For example, because I love quirky British cars that often feature poor ergonomics and weird functionality, I repress my common sense when it tells me to buy something more predictably conventional from Germany or Japan.

In usability terms, assume your customers/clients/visitors are *not* in love with your company/product/services. So at the very least, give them reasons to *like* you. And please note, just being quirky will not necessarily get people to love you. If you want the desired effect, make sure you identify the right cause!

This holder outside a sauna provides a convenient place to put your eyeglasses. Clearly, someone has thought through potential problems and has come up with a simple, yet welcome, solution at this luxury spa.

Multimodal experiences

Multimodal input and output has been a popular phrase among computer scientists since the 1950s. Here's what it's all about. Multimodal input to a computer includes keyboard, mouse, and voice. Multimodal output might include audible clicks, vibrations, and visual signals.

Multimodal experiences (my own phrase, I think) are when stuff asks me to switch interfaces in the middle of a task. These fall into three distinct categories:

▶ Switching from one routine to another within the same interface (all within the same app, website, or physical space)

▶ Switching from one routine to another within related interfaces (all online or all offline)

▶ Switching from one routine to another within unrelated interfaces (online to offline and vice versa)

This probably makes little sense at this point, so let me give you a bit more detail.

Switching from one routine to another within the same interface means that I can stay within the same browser window, within the same department at a store, or within the same wherever-I-happen-to-be in either reality or cyberspace (for example, buying dairy products and vegetables at the same supermarket).

Switching within related interfaces means moving from, say, a computer screen to a smartphone. Or from one store in a mall to another (for example, buying shoes one place and buying socks somewhere else).

Switching within unrelated interfaces means moving from your PC screen to a printout (for example, getting driving directions on your PC and printing them out so you can take them with you).

All three of these situations can be very good or very bad experiences, depending on how you choose to handle them.

Switching routines

The classic example of inconvenience is when a website has two interdependent forms that must be filled out separately. The story of booking movie tickets in Chapter One is fairly typical of this.

In the offline world, you know the situation all too well: You've waited in a long line only to be told that you should have been waiting in a completely different line. Getting switched from one person to another when phoning large companies is also an example. Think how many times you have to tell the same story before you finally get to someone who can actually help you.

Ideally, users should experience a seamless chain of events, each of which is perceived as bringing them closer to their objectives (this is a critical concept that I return to at the end of this chapter). The feeling of having to start over and over again is incredibly annoying and wildly frustrating.

Let me tell you a story that touches on many of the issues I've just mentioned.

Why I hate calling my bank

I used to have a bank in Florida. "Used to" is the operative phrase. Check out this transcript, which is not verbatim but is pretty close.

I had a question regarding my account. I found a phone number on my bank statement and made the call:

"Press One for blah, blah, blah. Press Two for silly advertisements. Press Three if you are clueless. Press Four for more options. Press Five if you would like this announcement in Spanish. Or stay on the line and a customer-service representative will be with you shortly." ["Shortly" at this bank is measured in very long increments.]

"Hello. All our customer-service representatives are busy. Please hold. Your call is very important to us." [But not important enough to staff up to help reduce the waiting time.]

"To help us provide better service, please enter the number of your account, followed by the pound sign." [OK. I have nothing better to do.]

"For your convenience, you can also visit us online at www.crappybank.com." [Er . . . I *called* you. Let's assume I actually want to *talk* with someone. Don't send me to a different interface.]

"We may record this call to monitor service quality. Would you like to participate in a survey after the call is completed?" [No. Let's just get things moving.]

"Thank you for holding. You will be served by the next available representative." [Another 15-minute wait.]

"Did you know that Atlanta-based Crappy Bank has 1,658 convenient locations?" [And apparently only one person manning the phones. Another 15-minute wait.]

"Hello, this is Greg. How may I help you?" [I confirm that this is actually a live human being and explain my problem.]

"Great. And what is your account number, sir?" [Er . . . didn't I already type that in?]

"Um . . . yes . . . um . . . we need this for security reasons. . ." [Are you assuming that from the time I punched in my account number on my phone until now that I was abducted by aliens and that you are no longer speaking to the person who initiated the call?]

"Can I have your Social Security number, please? And your mother's maiden name? And your shoe size?" [I guess Greg is just doing his miserable underpaid job.]

"And how may I help you?" [I explain again.]

"I'm sorry, I can't access that information from here. You'll have to call us again on Monday and ask for your personal bank advisor." *Click*. [Gosh, I have a personal bank advisor? I didn't know that. Does this person have a name? And a direct telephone number? Hello, Greg? Do you know . . . hello? Are you there? [Make myself a stiff drink. Make plans to close my account.]

Despite the fact that I tried to do things through the most convenient channel (for me, at least), the bank flummoxed me completely. In fact, after the better part of an hour on the phone, I was no closer to a solution than I was before. During these interactions, I was asked to:

▶ Switch interface (from phone to website)

▶ Wait in a different line (call again on Monday)

▶ Help address the site-owner's needs rather than my own (take the service survey)

And I was:

▶ Conned ("Your call is very important to us.")

▶ Presented with inappropriate/irritating content (info about online services)

▶ Lied to ("We need your number again for security purposes.")

I was also given the artificial feeling that I actually had some control over the situation (making menu choices, punching in my account number). In truth, I had no control and received no useful help.

So much for the "convenience of 24/7 hot-line support." Remember that convenience is *always* in the mind of the beholder. What may be convenient for you can be awful for your customers.

Switching interfaces

The whole notion of "one-stop shopping" is a really good, very convenient concept. But in the interest of online security, more and more streamlined operations are being derailed by odd security measures. As opposed to the bank, which suggested switching interfaces (from help desk to website), many e-commerce sites now force us to make an interface switch whether we want to or not. Here's another story of a failed interaction.

Here in Denmark, I have several international credit cards. One of them is particularly annoying when used online. When I enter my data on an e-commerce site, I am suddenly whisked away to a completely different site that asks various security questions and requires my unique password for the card. Only then can I return to the original e-commerce site. In at least one instance, I didn't make the return journey intact (I was timed out). As a result, I no longer use this card, which is certainly not good for the credit-card company's business.

I realize that many of you will say, "Oh, Eric is a nasty person. This card company is just protecting his interests." And this is true. Yet despite these security precautions, this remains the *only* credit card I have ever owned that actually *did* get hacked.

Real or imagined security issues are only part of the story. Often users are asked to provide additional data merely to satisfy the whims of the site owner (or stuff-owner. Did I just coin a word here?).

In the European Union, it is actually illegal to ask for information that is not *essential to task completion*. Even asking the gender of the user is off limits to marketers except when provided voluntarily. Businesses in the United States could learn something from this: The more information a website demands (required fields), the more anonymity is taken away, and the conversion rates fall because less typing means greater convenience. Let me repeat: Good usability is also good business. With the increased use of mobile phones in e-commerce, more and more site owners are discovering that their conversion rates plummet if they make people poke a smartphone more than absolutely necessary.

My point is this: Let people complete a task with the fewest possible distractions, detours, and derailments.

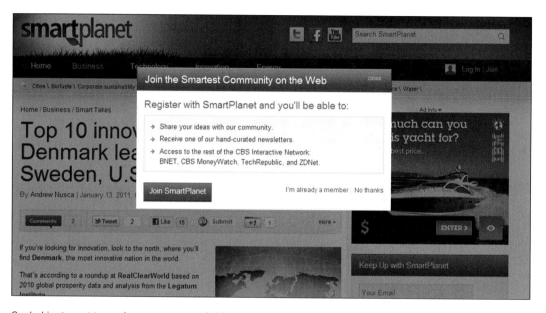

Gosh. I just want to read a news story and this site is doing its best to sidetrack me. Convenient? No way!

Well-meaning Skype has changed the publication dates for this rare book by Galileo into a telephone number! Very inconvenient, particularly if you don't know how to turn off this "helpful service." The site is that of the venerable auction house, Christie's, but the usability problem is actually Skype's.

Switching from on- to offline

Multimodality really becomes an inconvenience when we move from the online to offline worlds. A typical example online is when a website asks you to print out a form and fax it back. Honestly, I haven't owned a fax in over a decade. How many private people actually own fax machines these days? The possibility of scanning a printed document and e-mailing it back is an all-to-infrequent option.

One of the most prevalent problems is when information is accessed online but must be used in a completely different environment—for example, I have searched in vain for a site that can send driving directions directly to my phone, but I haven't found one (although many new cars automatically take information from a phone and put it in the car's navigation system). Another example is ordering movie tickets online, but then having to write down a transaction number so you can pick up the tickets 30 minutes before showtime. (Yes, this is how many of the goofy Danish movie theaters do things—and they even charge extra for this atrocious service.)

Many companies still don't quite believe that a simple barcode is sufficient proof of a transaction. "But what if the barcode is printed out several times? How will we know to whom it belongs? It could be stolen. It could be . . . I don't know . . . I don't like new technology." Hence, movie theaters in Denmark are slow to accept a barcode as a ticket; barcodes are only proof of purchase, and you must separately pick up the actual ticket . Yet a simple barcode is all that's needed to get me on most airplanes these days. You'd think the security issues were greater for someone about to board a 747 bound for New York than that same person about to watch Harry Potter board the Hogwarts Express.

Message: If you can't keep things within the same interface, at least use a little common sense.

Unfamiliar situations highlight convenience

From a usability POV, "convenience" issues are closely related to a classic problem: You never know you've left your umbrella somewhere until it starts to rain. And you never realize how few electrical outlets there are in public places until your smartphone runs out of juice. Travel in particular tends to bring convenience into focus, which is why there are so many references to hotels and airports scattered throughout this book.

When we venture into unfamiliar territory, we tend to look for comfort zones. That's because things that fit into our established personal routines provide exactly this kind of comfort. When they do, we think things are "convenient." Remember my earlier remarks? That we *like* someone *because*, and we *love* someone *despite*? Well, we *like* familiar routines, and whatever stuff we are designing for others should provide familiarity. Read more about this in Chapter Seven.

When I get to new hotels, I look for electrical outlets next to the bed. After all, my smartphone doubles as my alarm clock, but I also need to charge it while I sleep, and I don't want to stumble across an unfamiliar room to turn it off when it rings early the next morning. Although this is not an unusual use, you'd be surprised by how many hotels do *not* provide this convenience. In fact, out of some 30 hotels at which I stayed during 2011, less than 10 had electrical outlets next to the bed. Oh, yes, all of these hotel rooms had digital clocks, but I never trust myself to set them correctly. I prefer to remain within the comfort zone of my phone's alarm clock.

As designers and design evaluators, we *must* move out of our personal comfort zones. We can do this by enlisting the help of others when discussing usability. After all, designers tend to address their own needs first, but in doing so may miss the needs of others.[1] As evaluators, we must seek out alternative patterns of use.

A case in point: The iPod is one of the most successful pieces of electronic gadgetry to come out the past 25 years. And the "shuffle" function is brilliant for those who can't be bothered with playlists. But the iPod is built for pop music, not for classical works that comprise several movements. To add insult to musical injury, iTunes hasn't ever figured out that in classical music there may not be an "artist" per se, but that more specific bits of information are needed, such as the composer, orchestra, soloist, and conductor.

The burned wall in this toilet stall, which is just off the lobby of an otherwise classy Copenhagen hotel, suggests that the hotel should install either smoke alarms or ashtrays.

---

[1] Sorry designers, this is true—and it's what makes some of you good designers. If you were totally neutral, we could program a computer to do your work merely based on design patterns and best practices. Designers *need* to care. But caring also introduces prejudice.

Personas and other useful tools

To help avoid the problem of "designer ego," many design teams create user personas—fictional characters that represent archetypes (as opposed to stereotypes). Let me explain.

A stereotype (such as a marketing target group) is very general—for example, "Overweight, middle-aged men who want to lose weight without too much inconvenience." On the other hand, an archetype is specific—for example, "Jack is a slightly overweight 48-year old business analyst who is looking for a fitness center within a 10-minute drive from his home in suburban Chicago." When considering convenience (and other issues), archetypes are always much more useful. Here's why.

After you have four to eight personas (because you actually did some research and know something about your audience, right?), you can start creating task-based scenarios for these folks that outline what they want to accomplish while using your stuff (such as charging their phones while sleeping). Creating scenarios is *much* more difficult if you are working from stereotypes. Moreover, good personas help a design team focus: "Would Mary want to use this feature?" If "Mary" isn't interested, you had better be sure one of your other personas *is*. If not, you may end up creating more problems than you solve. Remember Alan Cooper's remark from the introduction: "When you hear 'someone might want this' you know you're about to hear a really bad design decision." This statement bears repeating, so I just did. By the way, Alan pretty much invented the persona concept.

Here's a quick caveat: You don't need a new persona for each new task. Many personas have multiple possible tasks. In my experience, if you have more than about eight personas, you are probably getting too specific and your archetypes will be less useful. However, once you have a good set of personas, it is easy to use these to develop other tools, such as scenarios (short stories that highlight what happens when a persona sets out to complete a particular task), or even customer journey maps that describe a range of related tasks.

Context is the kingdom

For years, the experts[2] have been telling us that "content is king." This is absolutely true. Without decent content, whatever stuff you have is worthless. A brilliantly usable website with page after page of fluff won't move market share. A gorgeous hotel won't get repeat visits if the beds are hard as rocks. Restaurants enjoy more success with good food than with classy cutlery.

But let's take things a step further to *context*—the way in which individual things are combined to create even greater value.

Like the electrical outlets in a hotel room, context is where the real design value lies in both the physical and virtual worlds. If content is king, context must be the kingdom.

---

[2]Designers, writers, bloggers, pundits, consultants, lecturers, and my friend Linda in Chicago.

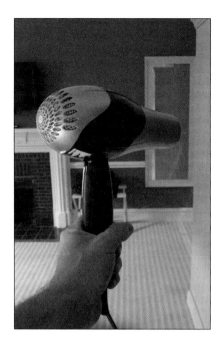

This hotel in Brighton, England was kind enough to provide a hair dryer. But the nearest electrical outlet was on the opposite wall from the only available mirror. (No, there was no plug in the bathroom.) The content was fine (mirror and hair dryer). But the context sucked.

On websites, a common style these days is to put tabs at the top of the page, lower-level navigational choices in the left-hand column, content in a wide middle column, and lists of related content (contextual links) in the right-hand column. Although this style doesn't adapt well to small-screen electronics, the concept of highlighting related content is incredibly important and provides real value. Unfortunately, although many designers "sell" this layout to their clients, far too many website owners fail to use this important facility. As a result, the right-hand column is often filled with nonsense—heaven forbid that we should waste valuable screen space!

Worse still, obviously related items, such as vacuum cleaners and the bags they use are not necessarily accessible from the same page. This is simply crazy. If you are investigating usability issues, be on the lookout for content that should be brought together, particularly when working on online stuff. Alas, during the rush to get a website launched, this is precisely the kind of work that gets put off until later and is eventually forgotten entirely. Believe me, creating these contextual groupings is *essential* for convenience no matter what you are building.

This bar has conveniently grouped all of the whiskeys, the vermouths, the white spirits (gin, vodka, and so on), and cognacs. Moreover, all the stuff needed to make a Bloody Mary is right there on the counter at the lower left. Some call this kind of categorization "information architecture." I call the result "useful."

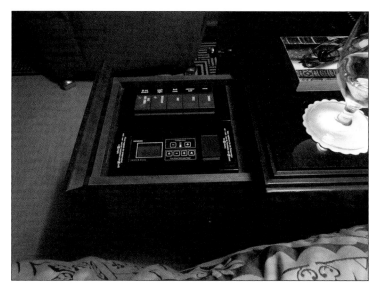

The brilliantly service-minded Hotel Adlon in Berlin, Germany provides convenient bedside controls for all the room lighting, the "do not disturb" lamp outside the door, and even nightlights at the touch of a button.

Make everything *people need* available

I'll get to the "just one click away" discussion in a moment. For now, let me suggest that you do every-thing you can to group things in a way that makes sense to the user. This is the second part of the dic-tionary definition I showed you at the start of this chapter: "Placed near at hand."

If you were fixing a car, you'd have all the tools you needed at hand, plus any parts that the repair would require. If you were preparing a meal, you would probably buy all the ingredients and have them ready before you started to cook. And if you were going to browse a subject on Amazon, you would collect all the needed links by opening them in a dozen or so browser windows.

Er . . . no. You wouldn't do this last thing. You expect Amazon to do the hard work for you by find-ing and making these links available. If you look at a typical Amazon page, you see that all the links and other information needed for checkout is gathered in one place, all the product information in another, and all the related links in a third. Amazon has nicely organized everything for you. It even uses different color backgrounds to help group related items so you know that they *are* related.

The takeaway? If someone is going to need content somewhere on your site, make sure it's easy to access.

The right-hand column from Amazon conveniently groups related items in colored boxes. All of these relate to purchase, exchange, and shipping of books, which is both quick and convenient.

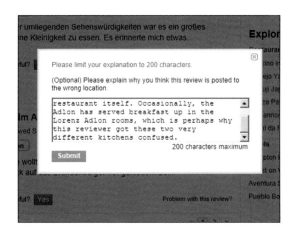

It would have been convenient if TripAdvisor had told me about the 200-character limit before I wrote my message. An automatic character-counter, like that used on Twitter, would have been particularly useful.

14. I am a U.S. citizen and want to take on Danish citizenship — will I lose my U.S. citizenship?

- Please see our section on Dual Nationality. It is possible that Danish immigration authorities may require you to give up your U.S. citizenship as a condition for granting Danish citizenship. An individual may exercise his/her right to formally renounce U.S. citizenship in accordance with INA Section 349(a)(5). Renunciation of U.S. citizenship, is a very serious and irrevocable exercise and should therefore only be undertaken after serious consideration of the consequences. This can be done at the Embassy by appointment only.

15. How do I obtain a certified copy of my U.S. birth/marriage/divorce certificate?

Please see our section on How to obtain vital records from the U.S. — please note that the Embassy cannot obtain records on your behalf.

This FAQ list from the United States Embassy in Copenhagen, Denmark provides a convenient contextual link at the start of question 15. But why is the section on Dual Nationality in question 14 not linked in the same way? Do you have similar inconsistencies on your website?

"Three clicks and you're dead"

We used to say this, of course, but today we know better. Not everything has to be three clicks away. Alas, the Internet remembers *forever*, which means that a lot of advice that used to represent best practice is still out there for you to find on Google, even though it is sadly out of date.[3]

Convenience and the *idea* of convenience go hand-in-hand. What has happened throughout much of the world these past few years is that people now have access to broadband. As a result, it takes much less time to download a web page to a PC. And 4G communications and high-speed wireless make it easy to download content to a phone or tablet, too—at least in some countries.

[3]The notion of best practice was popularized by Tom Peters and Robert H. Waterman in their best-selling *In Search of Excellence* (HarperCollins, 1982). Basically, "best practice" represents a method or technique that has consistently provided superior results and is therefore used as a benchmark.

So how does this play out? Well, not so many years ago, anything you clicked on a screen would cost you 10 to 30 seconds in waiting time. Therefore, people generally thought more carefully about *where* they clicked before committing themselves. Today, though, the clicks don't represent the same kind of time investment. I think this is why people seem to be more willing to click four, five, even six times to get to the content they want. But here's the catch: Each click needs to bring people closer to their goal. If it doesn't then users think they are wasting time, which is often the case.

Offline, the same is true: If you are transferred to another department when you phone a company and the transfer seems to bring you closer to your goal, you are generally pleased. It is only when you need to repeat the same story time and time again to different individuals that you get impatient and grouchy.

▶ **BUYING VACUUM-CLEANER BAGS SUCKS**
A TALE FROM THE TRENCHES

AS A DUTIFUL SON, I used to travel from my home in Copenhagen, Denmark to Miami, FL several times a year to run errands for my aging mom. A couple of years back, my mission was to buy replacement bags for her Sears Kenmore canister vacuum cleaner. No big deal . . . or so I thought. . . .

Alas, there was no bag in her vacuum: "It was full so I threw it out," she explained, which meant I had no stock number for this particular item and didn't even know what the bag looked like. But armed with the model number of the vacuum itself, I clicked on to the Sears website, full of confidence that I would emerge victorious from my online crusade with both a bag number and the address of the nearest Sears Service Center.

It took no time at all to find the vacuum model. But there was no link to a bag page. The product specifications were very sketchy; the contextual navigation on the page virtually non-existent. Oops. A sad state of affairs for the company that taught the world how catalog marketing worked.

Let the games begin.

I decided to turn things around and see if I could find the bags somewhere on the site and then trace them back to specific models. Well, the bags were indeed online, but the only information I could get was that they fit "selected Kenmore canister vacuums." No model numbers. No links. Nothing. Was my mom's vacuum one of the "selected" few? Who knew?

But there was an address for a service center not far away—and it was going to open at 9 AM a.m.—in about 15 minutes. Just to be on the safe side, I took a photo of the vacuum, wrote down the model info and hopped into the car, arriving just minutes after Sears had opened their doors to greet the customers they value so highly (it said so on the website).

On entering a huge, barn-like space, I was confronted with miles of washing machines and other appliances, but no vacuums. I sought help.

Sears rep: "Sorry. We don't sell vacuum-cleaner bags here. You'll have to go to a Sears outlet."

Me: "I thought this was a Sears outlet. . . ."

MORE >

▶ BUYING VACUUM-CLEANER BAGS SUCKS
A TALE FROM THE TRENCHES

Sears rep: "No. This isn't an outlet, it's a service center."

Me: "OK . . . so where is the nearest Sears outlet?"

Sears rep: "I don't know. I don't live around here."

Me: "Is there someplace you can look up the address?"

Alas I was too slow to ask this last question. The helpful Sears rep was already off to help someone else. Thankfully, a fellow frustrated customer came to my rescue and told me there was an outlet about 10 miles further down the road. I hopped back in the car and set off.

Although Sears Service Centers open at 9 a.m., their outlets don't open until 10 a.m. So I sat in the car and waited. When I finally got in, I grabbed a lifetime supply of bags since I didn't want to go through this rigmarole again. Was the online experience convenient? No.

Was the offline experience convenient? No.

About a year later, Sears finally fixed the website—sort of. Did they also fix their offline service? Don't ask me - I won't be going back anytime soon.

So far, so good. I found the vacuum. But not a word about which bags it uses. No joy under Specifications, Description, or Overview either. And no worthwhile contextual links.

▶ BUYING VACUUM-CLEANER BAGS SUCKS
A TALE FROM THE TRENCHES

"Designed to fit select Kenmore canister vacuums." Cool! But will this fit a Kenmore Model #28014? C'mon, Sears, give me a hint!

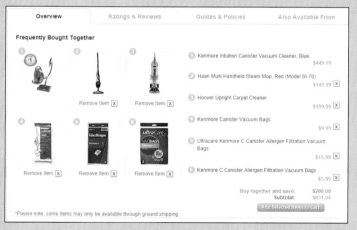

Sometime during the summer of 2011, Sears finally got wise and made significant improvements to the site. Now I can easily find the right bags, but for unknown reasons, *all* of the related items are pre-checked in the little boxes. Why Sears thinks I should buy three types of bag and a second carpet cleaner is beyond me. One inconvenience has been replaced by another—and has created a great opportunity to make lots of order errors.

TEN WAYS TO MAKE THINGS MORE CONVENIENT

1. Consider the tasks your users will be trying to complete. Without looking at your stuff, make a list of three things necessary for the completion of each task. Now look at your stuff. Are all of the things needed available to the user?

2. Can you group related content so it is easier to find?

3. Can you use colors or other visual signals to differentiate areas on an interactive page or device?

4. If you have multimodal experiences, can you make sure that the different processes don't get in each other's way?

5. How much do you know about the various users of your stuff? If you close your eyes, can you envision one of your users? If not, you need to know more about them. If you can see someone, create a quick persona, perhaps building on details from a real person you already know. Now go back to question 1 and ask yourself what this person would like to accomplish.

6. Can you eliminate unnecessary jumps from online to offline experiences? For example, letting people submit a form electronically rather than requiring them to print and fax a form.

7. Write down five reasons why a user should like your stuff. If these are difficult to identify, can you invent a few reasons? Now go back and figure out if anything is missing in terms of content or context that would make your new reasons viable.

8. Are you providing useful content? If not, what is missing? Opening hours? Contact information? Detailed product descriptions? Contextual links? Something else? Refer back to question 1 for inspiration.

9. Are you guilty of "For your convenience . . ." types of spin? If so, don't spin, fix!

10. Can you eliminate areas where users are forced to give you the same information several times?

OTHER BOOKS YOU MIGHT LIKE

The following books are something of a mish-mash of stuff I really like and hope you will read. All of these works provide unique insights related to convenience, but also much, much more. Please check them out!

▶ *In Search of Excellence*, Tom Peters and Robert H. Waterman, Harper-Collins, 1982.

▶ *WAYMISH: Why Are You Making It So Hard For Me To Give You My Money?*, Ray Considine and Ted Cohn, Waymish Publishing, 2000

▶ *Web Design for ROI*, Lance Loveday and Sandra Niehaus, New Riders, 2008

▶ *Contextual Design: Defining Customer-Centered Systems*, Hugh Beyer and Karen Holtzblatt, Morgan Kaufmann, 1998

▶ *The User Is Always Right: A Practical Guide to Creating and Using Personas for the Web*, Steve Mulder with Ziv Yaar, New Riders, 2006

THINGS TO GOOGLE

▶ Best practice
▶ Contextual enquiry
▶ Personas
▶ User scenarios
▶ WAYMISH

Chapter Five

Foolproof

Someone once remarked, "It's impossible to make anything foolproof because fools are so ingenious." [1] True as these words are, when it comes to usability, you still should attempt to "foolproof" your stuff, frustrating as this sometimes is.

Basically, you're trying to keep people from making mistakes and to give them a gentle push in the right direction when they need to do something. "Gentle" is the operative word because folks generally don't like being told what to do; I'll get back to this idea later in this chapter. That means you certainly don't want to get in their way while they're doing something—at least not in a way that they consider to be "pushy" or "intrusive." On the other hand, you want to make sure that they don't get into too much trouble along the way. Hence, your guidance needs to be as subtle as it is effective.

Achieving this kind of balanced experience is damned difficult, so consider yourself warned.

---

[1] No one is quite sure who said this first—Abraham Lincoln, Mark Twain, Martin Luther King—take your pick.

How the RAF can help win your battle

Over the years, I've relied on three key techniques to keep people out of trouble. Collectively, I refer to these techniques with the acronym RAF:

- ▶ Remind
- ▶ Alert
- ▶ Force

Remind simply points out that people may have inadvertently forgotten to do something, such as saving a document before closing it or attaching a file to an e-mail.

Alert means flagging and tagging stuff that specifically needs to be done before the user can move on, such as filling in a password or checking the "I accept your stupid terms of use" box.

Force means eliminating options that are not available, such as graying out menu items that cannot be used or are not appropriate at some particular point in time.

Much of this chapter deals with these three issues—what works, and what doesn't.

People forget to do stuff. So help remind them.

I recently upgraded my computer. My new operating system asks me *constantly* if I want to do something, or if I've remembered to do something. Although annoying, it has kept me out of trouble on several occasions—usually when I've forgotten to save a file.

I generally see two types of system reminders. The first is pretty standard: "Do you want to save your changes before closing this document?" I'm usually grateful for this help. The second, though, gets in my way and forces me to make a lot of choices: "There are unused icons on your desktop. Would you like to remove these?" (No! Go away and let me get on with my work). Alternatively, my computer asks redundant questions, "Do you *really* want to discard this document?" (Yes!) "Are you absolutely sure? This action cannot be undone." (If you ask me a fourth time, I'll discard *you*, you miserable machine!)

Anyway, the key is to be helpful, not to get in people's way by interrupting a smooth flow of events. Reminders that are not directly related to the task *do* get in people's way (such as cleaning up icons on the desktop—in most instances, people just want to start their computer and get on with things.) So, if you have reminders in your app or interface, either make them relevant to the task or get rid of them.

In the "real" world, we get all kinds of inappropriate messages that also get in our way. Voice mail systems that force us to listen to long advertising harangues before outlining the menu choices are depressingly common these days. And every car navigation system I've ever seen expects me to dismiss a screen of legal blather that reminds me that I should not look at the screen and drive at the same time. Frequently, I first notice this warning when I'm already driving, which actually makes the need to dismiss it a dangerous feature in itself.

In short, if help is not needed, stay out of the way.

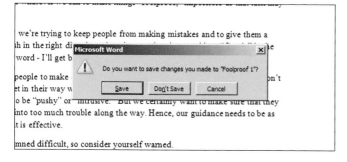

Oops. I forgot to save my document. Thanks, Microsoft, for reminding me!

No one wants to get home from the hardware store only to discover that they've forgotten to buy something they will soon need. This friendly reminder at a Home Depot warehouse in the United States provides a useful checklist for customers and undoubtedly also increases sales. A win-win situation.

Alerts and other warnings

Alerts are supposed to let you know of an error (such as a misspelled password), a change in state (such as a low battery), or something else that needs your attention. Unfortunately, some alerts simply insist that I acknowledge that my computer has done something—like a small child who constantly seeks approval. Let me give you an example.

One behavior I find particularly amusing (and particularly annoying) is when I plug earphones into my computer's headset jack or remove them. Invariably, the computer displays the following no-brainer messages:

"You've just plugged a device into the audio jack."

Duh. I know that. Very rarely does someone sneak up on my computer and plug something in without my knowing.

"You've just unplugged a device from the audio jack."

Er. . . OK. Either I accidentally unplugged something, in which case I would assume I'd notice that the sound was gone. Or I unplugged something on purpose, which makes the message completely idiotic.

The point is that preventing people from making mistakes is good. Irritating people by constantly stating the obvious is bad. As always, when designing these kinds of things, it's important to constantly assess their relevance to make sure they actually serve some useful purpose.

We seem to be much better about creating meaningful alerts in the real world. For example, cars have lots of lights to warn that oil pressure is low, the brakes are failing, a door is open, and so on. Many modern appliances provide the same functionality, such as refrigerators and freezers that warn if the temperature gets too high. And perhaps the best-known alert of all is the ringing of the phone.

My own rule of thumb is this: The more mission-critical something is (such as maintaining the temperature in a freezer), the more you need a method to let people know if something is amiss.

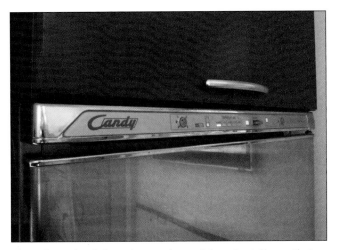

The red warning light at the top of my refrigerator tells me that the freezer is way too warm. Bad news if I need ice cubes. Good when I need a photo for a usability book.

This is LinkedIn's alert, telling me something is wrong with my login information.

What is the point of these two useless and irritating messages? Sometimes computer programs can be a bit too helpful.

The "boy who cried wolf" syndrome

Under all circumstances, beware of the "boy who cried wolf syndrome"—sending out so many irrelevant messages alarms and other notifications that when something really important comes along, people dismiss it out of habit without understanding that this time, their decision might have serious consequences. I've made this mistake many times myself when installing software—mindlessly clicking Next to get the process completed. Sometimes I miss something that I really should have paid attention to, such as where the new program will be located.

One of the other mistakes I often see is on e-commerce sites that flash small pop-up screens that tell me that my form has been accepted or some similar message. The idea of the pop-up is, in itself, not necessarily a bad thing. But if it looks exactly like a dialog box from your computer system, many people will wonder if they are talking to their computer or the application. In most instances, a dialog box indicates an error of some sort, so using this format for a more innocuous message can create unnecessary anxiety, particularly in less experienced individuals.

This message is actually from a website, asking me to confirm a purchase. Style-wise, though, it looks exactly like error messages on my computer, which is confusing.

Forcing the issue

Force, the third part of my RAF acronym, means that a program, application, or physical object refuses to let me do something inappropriate. For example, a car with automatic transmission, it's impossible to start the motor if it isn't in Park or Neutral. And many newer models also insist that the driver keep a foot on the brake simultaneously. The idea is to prevent the car from lurching forward or backward unexpectedly, which is entirely possible if a car has a manual gear shift.

In the world of computers, the technique of choice is to gray out menu options that are not available for some reason. For example, if you just saved your work, the Save option does not become available again until you have made a change to your document. Personally, I'm of two minds when it comes to showing people choices that aren't available. The problem is this: Sometimes what I really want to do is grayed out, and I simply don't know why. And I'm not alone. On countless occasions, I've seen people scream and yell at their computer out of sheer frustration with the limited menu options.

Of course, the alternative, making some things completely invisible, isn't really an answer either. That's because people wonder why a choice they've seen before is suddenly gone. In these instances, folks invariably click around, sometimes fairly aimlessly, in the hope that they will stumble across what they need. This is not good usability and it drives folks crazy. Incidentally, Albert Einstein is widely attributed as having defined insanity as "doing the same thing over and over again and expecting different results." Yet this is exactly what we do: click the same menu again and again hoping the choice we seek will magically reappear.[2]

When all is said and done, I think that graying things out is probably the better choice. However, in the future, I'd like to see programs also provide some explanation as to why a choice isn't active. For

---

[2] Although rebooting a smartphone two or three times does seem to help sometimes.

example, the program could display small instructional pop-up boxes on mouseover. But thus far, I haven't seen this implemented; there are undoubtedly even better solutions to be found.

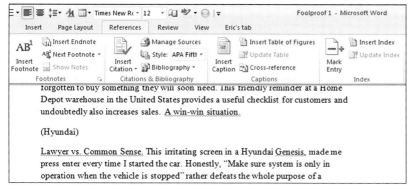

Several choices in this Microsoft Word menu have been grayed out. That's to let me know that these options aren't available to me at this particular moment. This is a typical example of how we can "force" someone's actions.

The dangers of personalization

Just to get our terms straight, personalization is what a computer or app does in the hope of satisfying our needs. Remembering a password or auto completion of an address in a form are two good examples of personalization. On the other hand, customization is what *we* do to a device so it suits our needs. This could be setting preferences in a word-processing program, changing our ringtone, or using a favorite snapshot as our "wallpaper."

For the most part, customization doesn't present a lot of usability problems, at least in terms of fool-proofing, because virtually all customization activities are things we do intentionally. But personalization is tricky—sometimes the program, app, or device does stuff that baffles us.

Adaptive menus that change according to what a website or app *thinks* we want to look at are a major headache. As computer software becomes more sophisticated, we're seeing more and more of these kinds of personalization tricks. But here's the rub: What interested me one time may not interest me the next. Here's an example.

Let's say I want to buy a car, so I visit the manufacturer's website. And let's say that the first time I'm there, I'm looking at compact cars and leasing options. But later, I find that it would be better for me to buy the car outright and that I can even afford a larger, better-equipped model. How does the app or website know that I'm no longer interested in cheap leasing options? If the menu choices have been changed to suit my earlier needs, I may have greater difficulty finding what I need during the second visit.

My feeling right now is that it is wrong to fiddle with the main navigation, but it can be beneficial to tweak the contextual navigation—and maybe even the primary content—to suit my needs. But let me be honest, the jury is still very much out on this issue as we just haven't had enough experience yet.

To summarize, try to keep your main navigation consistent, don't let personalization limit choices, and understand that *each visit* to a website or app is unique, even if the visitor has been there before.

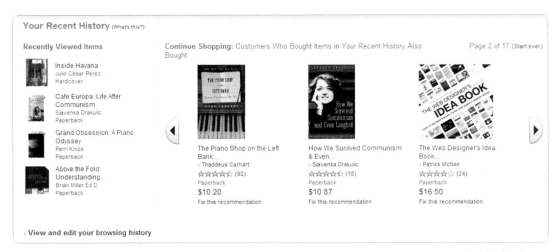

As opposed to customization, which is what I do to an interface by setting preferences, personalization is what a site or app does on its own accord to better suit my perceived needs. Here, Amazon.com has analyzed my recent browsing history and suggested related titles.

The magic of redundancy

Redundancy means giving people several similar options that complement each other, such as having both a phone number and an e-mail address. It can also mean repeating the same link or function in several convenient places, such as having a light switch at each end of a large room.

Usability experts agree that most people don't actually look at the "official" page navigation. Instead, they concentrate on information in the main content area—typically the middle column of a web page. That means if you want people to do something specific (such as buy your product), or if you think they are going to want to do something (such as download a PDF datasheet), make sure you have links right there in the content that are clearly visible, even if similar links are available elsewhere on the page.

Having said this, I hesitate to add that we saw a lot of this kind of behavior around 2005. Today, site visitors seem more likely to look at navigational options, particularly contextual links in a right-hand column. That said, the bottom of the page is a great place to repeat relevant contextual links for people who have read down to the bottom of a page of content—before they scroll back to the top of the page, get distracted by other things on the page, or just give up and go get a cup of coffee.

Redundancy is also important in terms of disaster recovery. For example, if you only have one channel through which you can talk to people, for example a contact form on a website, that channel is 100 percent mission critical. If it breaks down, you are out of business. But if you also provide a phone number or some other "human" element, a broken link won't necessarily deprive you of a sale (remember the jewelry store story from Chapter 1?). A simple e-mail address might be even easier. Or a chat option via a social media app like Facebook or Twitter. And if you also have a physical address, that gives people a pretty decent range of choices. When evaluating your stuff, anything that helps spread risk also improves your conversion.

Write helpful error messages

As I mentioned in the first chapter, some of the most useful alerts are the small messages that indicate that something is missing or incorrect within a form. In general, the more specific the alert message, the more useful it will be.

On many sites that require a login of some kind, if a person makes a mistake, the message simply reads, "Your login information is incorrect."

Because a typical login consists of both a username and password, this message would be more helpful if it would explain which of these two pieces of information are incorrect. A message such as, "This username does not exist. Perhaps your account is registered to another e-mail address" would be far better. Not only would I know where to start fixing the problem, but the application is even suggesting what may have gone wrong.

Providing hints and suggestions is always a good thing, although you don't want to go overboard. Try to keep your messages fairly short and to the point. You also want to keep the tone of voice friendly and use language people actually understand. That means avoiding the use of strange acronyms or technical language such as "Do you want to ADD the following certificate to the Root Store?" (I'm still not entirely sure what this means, but I see this message frequently. I ought to Google it . . . but I don't really care.)

In web development, it's not unusual to see a design team spend weeks agonizing over the text on the home page of a website, but leave the writing of the error messages to some hapless programmer. If you want to check this, type in the URL (web address) of any site (for example, `www.something.com`) and then add a slash and some nonsense text (for example, `www.something.com/asdf`). This will get you the infamous "404 Page Not Found" error. Read it. If it looks like it was written by a programmer, it probably was, which means you should probably check out what else was abandoned by the professional writers on the team. If you talk nicely to the programmers, they will print out an entire list of error messages for you. Happily, these are usually easy to change.

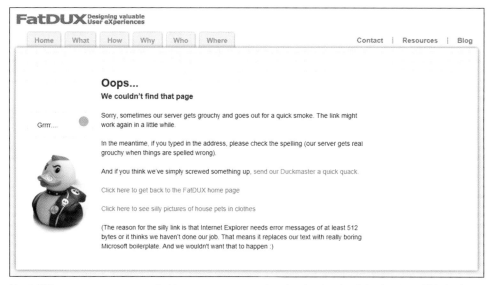

Most 404-error pages are created by programmers who plug in standard, boring text. This is the goofy page my company made—which, via blogs, became so popular, it actually won us two new clients.

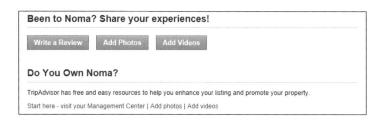

Standard, automatically generated messages, such as this one at the bottom of a page on TripAdvisor.com, can improve content quality . . .

. . . but the results can sometimes be disturbing. Human intervention and editing is not always a bad thing.

Helping people make better decisions

Most onscreen messages require me to make a decision of some kind. And even the ones that just want me to click OK mean that I have to consider what I'm actually approving. Keep in mind that I've been involved in programming and creating interactive programs since the late 1970s. But even so, I still encounter onscreen error messages that have me completely baffled (such as the ADD message I mentioned earlier). I figure that if I have problems making informed decisions, most of the world is going to be driven absolutely crazy. Here are a few simple questions you can ask yourself when evaluating onscreen messages:

▶ Do people know why the message appeared?

▶ Do they understand it?

▶ Do they know enough to respond intelligently?

▶ Is the information in the message helpful or confusing?

▶ Do people understand the consequences of this decision?

▶ Is the decision of an inexperienced person likely to be correct under the circumstances?

If the answer to any of these questions is "no" then you've got some fixing to do. If you are in doubt about something, ask someone. Assuming this person is not an experienced programmer, you'll probably get some good advice. By the way, I've observed that reactions usually vary according to age. My generation (the gray-haired baby-boomers) tends to worry that they will break something and are thus more careful about clicking. Conversely, the younger people are, the more likely they are just to go ahead and click and see what happens. In short, you'll probably identify more cognitive problems by asking older people. And if you *do* want to break an app, ask a teenager.

Not everyone can spll

One of the simplest ways to eliminate a lot of mistakes is to be forgiving of people who cannot spell or who inadvertently introduce a typo. This is most important when dealing with URLs.

Common errors include too many or too few Ws, for example

▶ `wwww.fatdux.com`

▶ `ww.fatdux.com`

It's pretty easy to fix this: Ask your hosting service to set up your server with what's known as a "subdomain wildcard (*)." They'll know what to do. Basically, the idea is that *anything* typed prior to your site's name redirects your visitors to the right page.

Also, simple spelling errors can also cause problems. For this reason, companies with odd names often register several different domain addresses and have all of them point to the correct URL. For example, the following are some variations from Mette Bødtcher, a former member of the Royal Danish Ballet, now a well-known designer of workout clothes for professional dancers:

- ▶ Bodtker
- ▶ Boedtker
- ▶ Boedcher
- ▶ Boedtcher

On a related note, if you have a search engine on your site, you might consider creating a thesaurus so that spelling errors or synonyms all lead to the right page. For example, you might want to indicate that the words "car," "auto," and "automobile" all mean the same thing and thus should lead to similar search results.

A good thesaurus, though, can take time to create and require specialized assistance from an information architect. What you can do as a quick fix is include various spelling errors in the keywords associated with a particular page.[2] This won't always help your internal search engine, but at least Google will know what to do when people make mistakes. If you are in doubt as to what spelling mistakes are occurring, check your query logs (the statistics that your server collects about your website). Here, you'll find all the high-volume, high-value, high-risk terms people are using so you can optimize for misspellings and synonyms. Search expert Rich Wiggins calls this the "Accidental Thesaurus."

People don't read instructions

As I mentioned a moment ago, people don't like long messages. They tend to tune out after the first sentence or two or as soon as they meet an unfamiliar word, acronym, or technical term. So, keep messages short and simple if you want them to work.

Don't expect people to read your instructions in detail. At best, they'll skim, mainly to see if whatever decision they're about to make is going to go very wrong. Just think how you reacted the last time you were asked to accept the Terms and Conditions of something. Like 99.99 percent of all people, you probably didn't read them. Instead you probably clicked the Accept box and moved on to the next step.[3]

For some reason, automobiles have incredibly detailed instruction books. In fact, some years ago, I did a word count on the driver's manual for a Mazda and discovered that it was 37 times longer than

---

[2] Keywords are one of three classes of what are known as metadata—data about data. This is the machine-readable stuff embedded in the code that enables Google, MSN, Mozilla and other search engines to find stuff on a website. The other two classes are Title (what you see written in the top bar of your browser and as the link on a Google results page) and Description (the 140-character description that you see in a page of search results).

[3] The Terms and Conditions for Apple's iTunes babbles on for about 40 printed pages, representing more than 17,000 words that only a lawyer could love. iTerms?

the United States Constitution. This came as something of a surprise to me. Up until this time, I had assumed it was tougher to build a nation than drive to the supermarket.

Basically, car owners want to know the correct tire pressure and maybe something about what kind of oil to put in the engine and how to check the various fluids. Apart from that, the rest of these books are pretty useless. I discovered this with a rent-a-car a few years ago when I simply could not figure out how to open the cover to the gas cap. I never did figure it out and ended up returning the car when it was running on fumes.

Cover-Your-A** legal language is really what most instruction books are about these days (Terms and Conditions, too). American ads on radio and TV are particularly curious in this regard as the legally required text is either rattled off so fast that it is impossible to understand, or printed in text so small that even the person who wrote it would have trouble reading it aloud. Although I know that laws must be followed, if you can avoid this kind of nonsense, you will be better off and your usability will undoubtedly improve.

Quite simply, if you write instructions, write them as if you actually expect someone to read them and act on them. Instructions should instruct, not demonstrate that your lawyer has practiced due diligence.

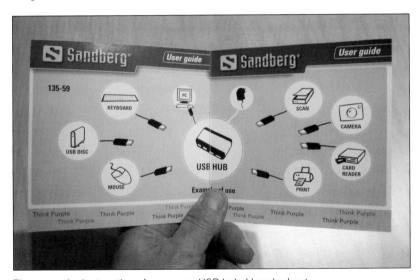

These are the instructions for my new USB hub. I laughed out loud when I opened the folder. Absolutely idiotproof!

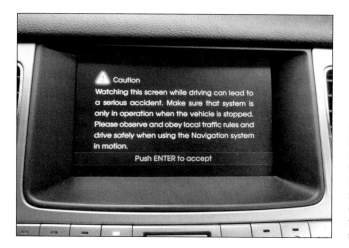

Lawyer versus Common Sense. This irritating screen in a Hyundai Genesis made me press ENTER every time I started the car. Honestly, "Make sure system is only in operation when the vehicle is stopped" rather defeats the whole purpose of a navigation system! And, the last line of the text actually contradicts the previous sentence. Who writes this nonsense?

Don't make people memorize your messages

A lot of alerts, reminders, and other messages appear in pop-up windows that disappear when clicked. One of the big problems is that occasionally, these pop-ups contain information that is needed some-where else on a site—or even on a different device—so make it "portable." Let's face it: People won't always remember your instructions or information, so don't ask them to. Here are two of the classic mistakes.

The first has to do with forms. Let's say you've just filled out a long page full of details and clicked Submit. The next page tells you that you forgot to enter your phone number and some other details (see the "Tale from the Trenches" about the NAACP in Chapter 1). So, you hit the back button and try to make the machine happy.

Oops. Suddenly there's no reminder of what was wrong; the page looks exactly like it did when you submitted it. You try to remember as much of the error message as possible and click Submit a second time to see if you managed to correct everything. Let me be frank, this is not a particularly foolproof way to get people to comply with the needs of your form. Again, don't make people remember your messages or instructions.

The second classic mistake is putting information in a pop-up box that must be written down or cut-and-pasted into something else. Sometimes order numbers and even registration numbers appear in this manner, which is completely crazy. This kind of information should be somewhere much more permanent, and it should probably be supplemented with an e-mail confirmation.

Avis Rent-A-Car is particularly good about asking people to print out specific pages related to their booking. What's more, in order to save paper, they even give you the option of *not* printing all the legalese that you aren't going to read anyway. And finally, they also send an e-mail. Not a bad way to ensure that people have their paperwork in order—although there shouldn't be a need for any paperwork at all thanks to Quick Response (QR) codes and text messages.[4]

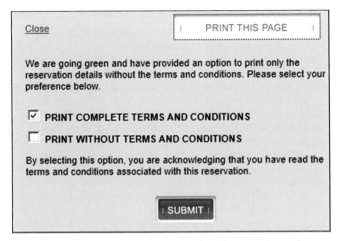

This pop-up window from Avis Rent-A-Car gives me the option to print my booking details without all the useless legalese.

Why use paper at all? QR codes can be sent to smartphones to confirm reservations, tickets, and so on. Or they can be scanned by phones to provide direct links to relevant subjects. Here's one printed in a Danish magazine advertising dairy goods.

[4]A QR code is a small, square digital barcode that is easily read by a smartphone or displayed on a small screen. QR codes on mobile phones are now replacing traditional boarding passes at many airports.

Sometimes you *do* have to state the obvious

Some years ago, I had lunch with a senior technical writer at Philips Electronics in the Netherlands. He told me he was reviewing various user manuals and trying to clean up the language. Before he started, he'd spent quite a bit of time with the Philips help-desk people, trying to identify the key questions he needed to answer—the kind of stuff we now find in good quick start guides that take the "need to know" information from the user manual and print it in a few convenient pages.

To his surprise, my friend discovered that an awful lot of people simply forgot to plug in their TV, DVD, or CD player. In fact, in my own enthusiasm to get something unpacked and see it work, I've also forgotten to plug stuff in; it's a more common mistake that you might think. So, the Philips troubleshooting guides now start with "Is the device plugged in and the power switched on?" And last I heard, calls to the help desk are down.

People don't remember things from one time to the next

In Part Two, "Elegance and Clarity," I spend a lot of time showing you ways to make stuff more intuitive. But as some of these techniques also relate to the subject of foolproofing, I figure I'll kick-start the discussion here.

Because people generally don't read instructions, designs need to send out strong signals to tell people what they need to do at any given time. Unfortunately, we designers tend to think our elegant solutions are more obvious than they often are. Here's the bottom line: Even if people have figured out how to use something once, there is no guarantee that they will remember the next time they use it.

We tend to learn things in one environment and expect to be able to use these skills in similar environments. For example, airports have signage that is pretty standardized. The planes are at "gates," the gates are numbered, and grouped along corridors labeled "A," "B," "C," and so on. After you've figured out one airport, you can pretty much find your way around most other airports.

Websites should work the same way, but they won't if a design team gets "creative" or "innovative" and invents new, unusual ways to accomplish various tasks. Don't count on people's memory to save a quirky design solution.

I've made this same mistake twice now, incorporating home-grown blogging tools that are "native" to my company's content-management system. The first time I did this, it was with an open-source CMS. The second time was with an expensive proprietary system. Neither blogging solution matched the best practices established by the major players, such as Blogger and WordPress. As a result, new bloggers in our company need a lot of instruction to use our current tool, and no one remembers how to work it the next time they need it. These two mistakes have cost our company thousands of dollars as well as goodwill because our blogging tends to be very irregular (who wants to be bothered with it?). I will not make this mistake a third time!

My advice? Make your stuff predictable and make routines repeatable. As usability guru Steve Krug says, "Don't make me think!"

Physical deterrents

Much of this chapter has been devoted to online (or at least screen-based) applications. However, there are various ways to foolproof stuff within the physical environment, too. The most effective of these methods is to adopt a physical deterrent.

Baggage carts on the escalator are dangerous. These simple barriers at an airport allow standard rolling luggage to pass easily, but keep out the carts.

Basically, most physical deterrents fall into one of five categories. Stuff that:

▶ Reminds us that we are about to do something bad

▶ Negates the value of whatever bad thing we want to do

▶ Forces us not to do something bad

▶ Causes us inconvenience if we don't behave

▶ Causes us pain if we don't behave

Examples of the first instance, are often found in traffic management. In the U.K., the streets are clearly marked "Look left" or "Look right" at pedestrian crossings. I assure you, this is not just for the benefit of the tourists: London traffic is so complex that even the natives need reminding from time to time.

The crosswalks in London are marked "Look Right" and "Look Left," which I've been told saves the lives of tourists and natives alike.

We also know the effect of speed bumps or changes in street surfaces is to wake sleepy drivers if they drift into the opposite lane or keep bicyclists on their paths. And of course, we have signs, although there are invariably people who overlook these; a sign is easier to ignore than a speed bump.

Physical size can also act as a deterrent. Big fat fobs on old-fashioned hotel keys were supposed to keep people from running off with them. Gas station restrooms often have a key tied to a huge hunk of wood for the very same reason. This solution is less collectable than a brass fob, but equally effective—or perhaps more so precisely *because* it isn't collectable.

Big keys and big key fobs help keep people from walking off with them inadvertently. I hasten to add that all of these keys were gifts from others . . . even the Men's Room key. It's a long story. . . .

As to negating the value of an action, security tags in stores are a classic example. Not only will most of them trip an alarm if someone tries to walk out with stolen goods, but some actually explode, spreading indelible ink on clothing and other items the moment someone tries to remove them without the proper equipment. The basic idea is that whatever someone is thinking of doing is just not worth the risk or bother.

Forcing us to behave usually means introducing various physical obstacles that prevent a particular action. Typical examples include the cut-off corner of the SIM card in our telephone, which prevents it from being inserted incorrectly. Gates and bars across walking paths make it difficult for bicyclists to ride where they're not supposed to. And simply keeping various controls out of sight or under lock-and-key generally prevents people from messing with stuff they shouldn't, such as access to certain floors from an elevator in a public building.

Closely related to "force" is "guiding." Here, specific paths, such as one-way streets, barriers at rock concerts, and guard railings at Walt Disney World, help keep people moving in the same direction to eliminate mistakes and improve flow.

Inconvenience deterrents slow us down in some way. Not like speed bumps, but more like "If you really want your McBurger® without onions, it is going to take an extra 10 minutes." Slowing down fast food is a good way to encourage compliance, even if it isn't necessarily hard-core foolproofing.

And as to stuff that causes us pain, well, we've all seen broken glass lying along the top of a wall. Or razor wire at the top of a prison fence. These are some of the clearest physical deterrents. I once saw a photo in a 1937 *National Geographic Magazine* from the Berlin Zoo. Huge, ugly spikes kept the elephants from running off. Today, we'd never use this in a zoo—only the Nazis could think of something this cruel. But we do use tire spikes at rent-a-car agencies so folk aren't tempted to run off with a Chevy.

Today, we'd call this solution cruel. But in Hitler's Berlin, this was acceptable as a deterrent, keeping Jumbo in his place at the Zoo. Today, we use spikes to stop cars, not animals. The photo is by Douglas Chandler and was featured in the February 1937 issue of *National Geographic Magazine*.

▶ EXPLODING CHICKEN ALFREDO
A TALE FROM THE TRENCHES

I LIKE TO COOK. But I admit to being lazy, and after a long day at the office, I'm not always eager to spend a lot of time in the kitchen. This is particularly true when the family is out and I will be dining alone. All hail the magic microwave!

Back in 2005 or thereabouts, I came across a great line of microwavable Italian meals. Now, like most men, I tend not to read instructions. When it comes to microwave food, though, timing is critical, so I looked at the package of my frozen Chicken Alfredo to find out what I needed to do.

Although the instructions were in no fewer than seven languages, which should make things pretty foolproof throughout a large part of Europe, I noticed something else that looked like a problem in the making: The instructions were divided into three main sections:

- ▶ Cooking instructions
- ▶ Conventional oven
- ▶ Microwave oven

Under "Microwave oven," the first line read, "Place bowl in microwave." Of course, I know enough to poke holes in the protective film first. But I wondered why this wasn't mentioned as the first point. As it turned out, upon careful reading of the microscopic text on the package, I saw that it *was* mentioned—up at the top under "Cooking instructions."

The problem is that there was a fatal disconnect in the instructions. The instructions that were common to both cooking in a conventional oven and a microwave were collected at the beginning of the text: "Remove outer sleeve and pierce film with a fork. Ensure product is hot before serving." Yet most people reading the instructions would immediately jump past these remarks to read about conventional or microwave cooking, depending on their specific needs. In other words, it was easy to miss a critical piece of information.

Naturally, I called the U.K.-based producer to hear if they knew about this problem. Doesn't everyone do this? Of course you do!

Amazingly, I actually was put right through to the product manager for this food line. But after the introductory pleasantries, and before I had a chance to explain why I had called, he told me, "I'm glad you like our product, but actually we're withdrawing it from the market. We don't know why, but our packaging seems to explode in the oven."

▶ EXPLODING CHICKEN ALFREDO
A TALE FROM THE TRENCHES

I told him I might know why. He changed the packaging. The company was later sold. And the product was dropped. *C'est la vie.*

Microwavable Chicken Alfredo. Just the thing for an easy meal when the family is gone for the evening. . . .

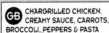 **CHARGRILLED CHICKEN, CREAMY SAUCE, CARROTS, BROCCOLI, PEPPERS & PASTA**
COOKING INSTRUCTIONS:
Keep frozen until ready to use. These are guidelines only. Remove outer sleeve and pierce film with a fork. Ensure product is hot before serving.
CONVENTIONAL OVEN:
- Preheat oven to 350°F / 180°C / Gas Mark 4.
- Place bowl on a tray in the oven centre.
- Cook for 30- 35 minutes.
- Remove film immediately and serve.
MICROWAVE:
- Place bowl in the microwave.
- Heat on full for 6½ mins (750W/D).
- Remove film immediately.
- Stand 1 minute.

So, what's the first thing I need to do if I'm going to warm this in the microwave? Did you say "Put bowl in microwave"? Most people do. But actually, the instructions at the beginning tell me to first remove the outer sleeve and pierce the film with a fork. Oops . . . this is a recipe for disaster.

MORE >

▶ EXPLODING CHICKEN ALFREDO
A TALE FROM THE TRENCHES

So for fun, I now put CDs in the microwave. They put on an amazing show, but don't taste very good.

WARNING My lawyer tells me to tell you not to try this at home. So come to my home and I'll zap one for you. Or give this book a nice review on Amazon and I'll send you a personalized zapped CD in the mail. Supplies are limited.

Just thought you'd like to see what a CD looks like after I've zapped it in the microwave.

TEN SIMPLE WAYS TO MAKE STUFF (FAIRLY) IDIOTPROOF

1. Can you give people several different ways in which they can respond so if one thing doesn't work, they still have an alternative?

2. Did you find any error messages or instructions that you needed to read twice to understand? If so, there's an opportunity to improve your written communications!

3. Can you speed up response times so that people are not likely to repeat an action (like the story in Chapter Two in which I ordered three Rolls-Royces)?

4. Can you build in a physical deterrent, such as a child-proof cap, barricades, or some other technique to prevent people from harming something—including themselves? Do you know *what* the harm could be? You can't prevent harm without understanding it first!

5. Do you have error messages or alerts that could be confused with system warnings? If so, can you create a more unique design for these? Or even eliminate these messages entirely?

6. Are you doing anything "helpful" that is actually getting in people's way as they try to accomplish the task at hand?

7. Does your stuff include personalization features, such as adaptive menus, that could cause confusion by remembering behaviors that may not be relevant the next time someone uses something?

8. Are you providing cognitive clues and guideposts to point people in useful directions as they interact with your stuff?

9. Have you kept instructions to a minimum? Have you made sure that information (such as confirmation numbers) is available *when* and *where* people actually need it?

10. Is someone's idea of a "foolproof solution" actually worse than the problem it was designed to solve? If so, can you smooth out the roughest edges or perhaps even drop the solution entirely?

OTHER BOOKS
YOU MIGHT LIKE

There are actually only one book in this section, the second suggestion isn't even a real book. Rather, it is a collection of cards that illustrate 101 patterns for influencing behavior through design. Absolutely brilliant!

> *Search Analytics for Your Site*, Louis Rosenfeld, Rosenfeld Media, 2011.

> *Design with Intent: 101 patterns for influencing behavior through design*, Dan Lockton with David Harrison and Neville A. Stanton, Brunel University/Equifine, 2010.

You can download these cards free of charge at http://www.danlockton.com/dwi/Download_the_cards

THINGS TO
GOOGLE

> Bad error messages
> Error messages for security features
> Metadata
> QR code
> Design with intent
> Accidental thesaurus

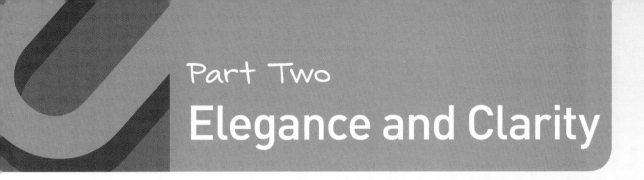

Part Two

Elegance and Clarity

The next five chapters deal with psychological parameters. Assuming that everything actually works as it should in physical terms, your job now is to make sure that things do what people *expect* them to do.

The trick is to avoid surprising people. In the usability business, surprises are almost always negative, "Ooh. Why did it do that?" or "Where did *that* come from?" or "Everything was going so well. But what am I supposed to do now?"

Service-design folks will preach to you about the glories of helping your customers embark on "a journey of discovery." And a "discovery" is good—but very different from a "surprise." Discovery generally represents an added bonus, often in the form of new information. But a surprise usually causes a change in perception toward something that you already thought you had figured out. Hence, surprises can be disconcerting.

What's in this part?

We'll be examining the following aspects of "elegance and clarity":

- ▶ Visible (I can actually *see* stuff)
- ▶ Understandable (I know what I'm looking at and get how it works)
- ▶ Logical (the stuff I see and the procedures I am asked to follow make sense)
- ▶ Consistent (the rules of the game won't change on me unexpectedly)
- ▶ Predictable (when I do something, I have a clear idea what's going to happen next)

As you've probably figured out by now, a lot of usability issues are relevant in more than one category. For example, if something strikes you as illogical, then it probably isn't particularly understandable either. I've done my best to put things into what I think are sensible categories. Please forgive me if I've done things differently than you would have. There are no right or wrong ways to do this so feel free to adapt my advice to suit your needs.

Chapter Six

Visible

"If a tree falls in the forest and no one is around to hear it, does it make a sound?" This thought experiment was suggested by Pastor George Berkeley, an Anglo-Irish philosopher, in his 1710 work, *A Treatise Concerning the Principles of Human Knowledge.*[1]

Of course, Berkeley was pondering the existence of a "higher being," which people will debate from now to eternity. But when it comes to interactive media, there is a very clear answer: If an object is not seen or acknowledged, it simply does *not* exist. Let me be blunt here: If a link isn't recognized as a link, folks won't click it. If an option isn't recognized by someone, it doesn't exist.

This is why this chapter is entitled "Visible." Visibility is one of the most important elements when it comes to creating "elegance and clarity."

---

[1]Prior to Berkeley, John Locke suggested that we must accept a materialistic philosophy. But Berkeley cleverly did away with materialism and suggested it was all a mind game. Later, David Hume's theories turned everything on its head. Believe it or not, all of these 18th-century philosophical theories are directly related to how we perceive websites and other interactive devices. And here you thought a liberal arts education was a waste of money. . . .

I'm always surprised at how many *un*usable "improvements" car manufacturers make. For example, the controls needed to adjust the side mirrors on this Nissan are completely hidden from view. Usually, I expect to find them on the driver-side armrest.

Oh, there are the controls! They're hidden at the bottom of the dashboard, behind the steering wheel. How practical. "Yes, officer, I am planning to move my car . . . just need to take a photo for a book . . . "

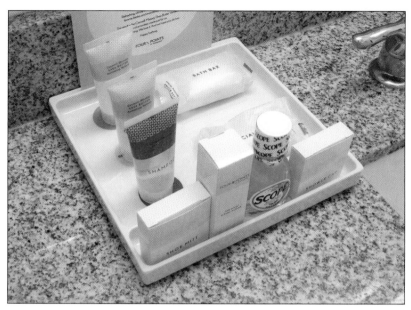

The Sheraton Four Points hotel in Savannah, Georgia provides a good array of complementary toiletries . . .

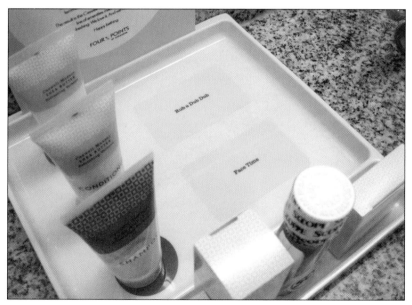

. . . and underneath, there is a delightful "reveal" as phrases come into view that relate to the object you just picked up. Not only does this help housekeeping keep the tray nicely arranged, it provides guests with a pleasant little discovery.

Four ways things become invisible

I firmly believe that if you cannot see something you are looking for—or ought to be aware of—you have encountered a serious usability problem. And if you're designing stuff, don't assume that people are going to play mind-reader, have the patience (or presence of mind) to click around looking for important supplementary information, read the fine print in your Terms and Conditions, or do something else that could radically affect their customer journey.

Things become "invisible" when needed information:

▶ Is not available where people are looking.

▶ Is physically blocked by something else.

▶ Is not recognized even if it is in plain view.

▶ Simply doesn't exist.

There are trees falling silently in forests a million times a day. This chapter is going to help you make them noisy again.

First-time visitors to this well-known Danish company have to think fast if they want to find the reception area. It's in the first line on this incredibly unusable sign—shortened to "Recp." for extra clarity, particularly for the company's many foreign visitors.

The Danish importer of this excellent curry paste from Patak's in the U.K. stuck on a big, white label with a translated list of ingredients. This apparently satisfies the legal needs of the Danish Ministry-of-something-or-other. But it obscures the cooking instructions, which are only in English. #whodreamsthisstuffup?

The mysterious "fold"

Back in the days when newspapers were printed in "broadsheet" format, they were folded for display at the newsstand. Hence, only half of the information printed on the front page was actually visible until someone picked up the paper and unfolded it. The rest was said to be "below the fold."

Today, the newspaper industry is rapidly adopting the tabloid format, which is smaller, but displays the entire front page of the newspaper because it isn't folded.

When the first websites started to appear, the concept of "the fold" took on new meaning. "Below the fold" meant all the stuff that wasn't immediately visible unless the visitor scrolled down the page. Many uninformed designers still think that people don't scroll, which is nonsense (more about that in a moment). But although the reasoning is faulty, the fold *does* exist and we therefore need to acknowledge it. The tricky part is that unlike a physical newspaper, the precise position of the "fold" in a browser window is impossible to pin down.

The two leading daily newspapers in Denmark have both received design awards. *Berlingske* has adopted the more modern "tabloid" format, while *Politiken* has stuck to broadsheet. Curiously, *Politiken* chose to move the headline below the fold, which must rank as one of the dumbest design decisions in the history of journalism.

People *do* scroll!

Most design teams think people don't scroll. Yet starting in 1996 we began to see a steady stream of research that proves that people *do* scroll. In fact, a Global Solutions Newsletter prepared by Razorfish in the spring of 2008 showed that more than 75 percent of readers scroll before they do anything else on a page! That's because they feel compelled to scan the content to get their bearings. Most scroll at least 50 percent of a page.

Have you ever visited Wikipedia.org? The chances are you have. Did it ever cross your mind how often you scrolled? Probably not. I rest my case . . . almost.

Recently, I printed out roughly two dozen "pages" from Amazon.com. These represented a cross-section of books, DVDs, and physical objects. The average printed length of these pages came to roughly 14 A4 sheets of paper. (A4 is a little narrower and a little longer than U.S. Letter format.) Wow. Fourteen pages! Clearly people scroll—a lot! If you don't believe this, print out some pages yourself. And if you still think scrolling is bad, write to Amazon and let me know what Jeff Bezos says when you tell him his website is useless.

Why we can't pinpoint the fold

There are several reasons the fold is tricky to locate:

> ▶ **The position of the fold depends on the size of the browser window.** If you have a big screen and maximize the browser window, you'll see more of any given web page. But if you decide

to make the window smaller, you'll see less of the page. And on a smartphone or netbook, the maximum viewing area is always smaller than that visible on a full-size computer monitor.

▶ **Each time a new toolbar is opened, the fold moves higher up on the page.** Toolbars are those helpful rows of functional icons that appear at the top of your browser window. They give you fast access to various features, such as Print and Save. But the more of these toolbars you open, the more space they fill in your browser window. Hence, the web page gets shoved further down, which places the fold higher.

▶ **The lower the screen resolution, the higher the fold**. Screen resolution can change what you see in a browser window dramatically. Even though there is general agreement that a standard resolution these days is 1028 × 760 pixels[2], folks with poor eyesight often change their screen resolutions to something much lower—typically 800 × 600 pixels. This also changes the amount of data visible in the browser window.

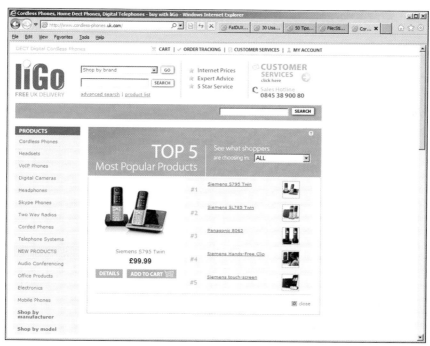

With only a small number of toolbars open, this is what the LiGo website looks like.
Note the bottom two menu items on the left: Shop by manufacturer and Shop by model.

---

[2]A pixel is the itty-bitty colored square that represents the smallest digital unit on your screen. If you use a magnifying glass, you'll see that everything on your screen is made up of these tiny squares.

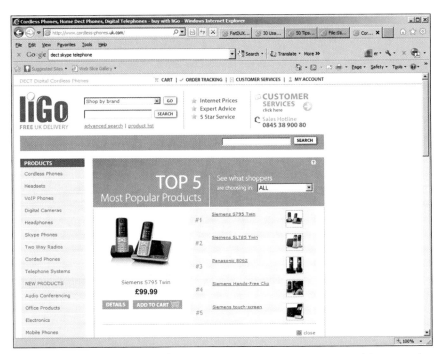

Oops. Open a couple of toolbars (including the status line at the bottom of the screen) and suddenly the menu gets shorter as the fold moves higher. Yet very little on the page suggests that I'm not seeing the full menu.

Change the screen resolution to 800 × 600 pixels and you see even less of the same screen. That pesky "fold" has moved again—also horizontally.

Actually, the LiGo website has a pretty long homepage. Some of this stuff is undoubtedly there because it might help search engine optimization. But most human visitors will never see it as it is well below the fold on a page that doesn't visually signal that scrolling is necessary.

When the fold is important

Remember those "trees falling in forests"? Well, we want people to see important stuff with the least amount of effort. On a website, this means that when people land on a page, we want all the important functions right at the top of the page where they can easily spot them.

Here is a short list of stuff that should absolutely be above the fold:

▶ Branding and main navigation

▶ Helpdesk contact information

▶ Internal search box

▶ Link to shopping carts and checkout

▶ Link to Contact

▶ Facilities to change the language

▶ Key input areas in rapid-fire apps (such as a currency converter)

▶ Key output areas (keep these near the input areas)

The following is the stuff you can (usually) safely put at the bottom of your page:

▶ Legal notice

▶ Privacy policy

▶ Physical address and phone number

Like all things, these lists have exceptions. Perhaps the key one is the placement of the address and phone number. If you are a commercial operation and depend on people calling you or visiting your place of business, your phone and address should be visible above the fold. These days, a lot of folks use smartphones to look up addresses, so the idea is to keep stuff that is important as visible as possible. But if you're a design agency, your physical address might be less important, so why waste valuable space at the top of the page?

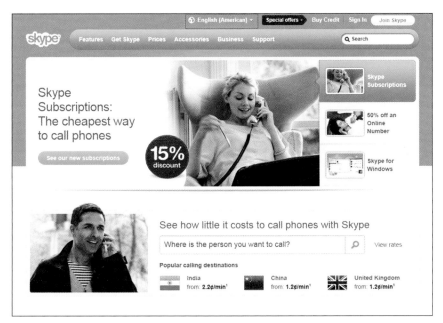

Here's the standard Skype start page. Notice the language button right at the top where it's easy to spot . . .

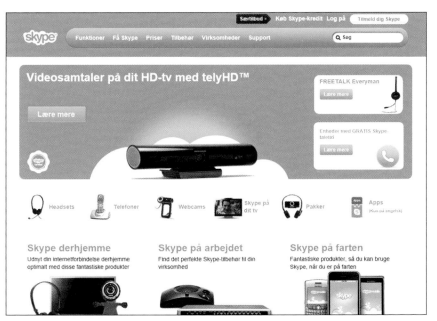

. . . until you click Accessories. The Skype webshop looks at my computer, figures out it is located in Denmark, and automatically switches the default language. To complete the confusion, choice of language is moved to the bottom of the page where it is truly out of sight. Oops.

When the fold *isn't* important

Let me just share a couple of quick observations that are based on years of detailed industry research (no, I'm not being facetious).

First, it's impossible to pinpoint the fold. No matter what your best guess is, you're probably only going to satisfy about 10 percent of your visitors.

Second, make your page "scroll-friendly" so you don't have to cram as much as possible near the top of the page. (More about this in a moment.)

Finally, many of you are going to have advertisers who insist on seeing their messages above the fold. But the truth is, if a page is scroll-friendly and features compelling content, ads at the *bottom* of a long page actually enjoy click-through that is as good as or better than an expensive banner ad at the top.

So, what's the takeaway from this long discussion? Well, you need to recognize that there is a fold and that it has a major effect on the visibility of objects on your page. But don't get too hot and bothered about the fold's precise location. You need to think "scroll-friendly."

Typical banner placement. Most people ignore these ads and jump right to the main content area. If folks see these ads at all, it's generally after they're done looking at editorial stuff—and after they've scrolled past the noise at the top of the page. That said, because the content columns are staggered, this is a fairly scroll-friendly solution.

Creating scroll-friendly pages

A couple of chapters ago, I mentioned the concept of scent—designing stuff so people are given some cognitive clues as to what they should probably do at any given point in their interactive journey. Creating scroll-friendly pages means that the layout of a page sends out a strong signal that the user should scroll beyond what is currently visible on the screen.

Traditional graphic designers *hate* this, but the trick is to knock stuff out of alignment. In other words, wherever that devilish fold happens to fall, you want your layout to cut through an element (for example a picture) so that the visitor knows that there is more to see if he scrolls.

To achieve this misalignment, you need to give up the notion that stuff should be lined up horizontally. Instead, let each column on a web page live its own life, so to speak. This means that when a page is viewed as a single unit, the visual designers scream bloody murder. As is so often the case, what works well in print doesn't always translate well to the screen—at least if we are concerned about usability.

The trick to scroll-friendliness is to cut off content at graphically dumb places. My own rule of thumb is this: The cleaner the lower edge of your web page looks, the less scroll-friendly it is.

Unfriendly scroll-friendly pages

Now, let's assume you have a design that sends out all the right visual signals. But let's also assume that the design physically separates two pieces of related information. This can also create problems. For example, if I am asked to submit information in a box at the top of a page—for example in a currency converter—I want the output to be in the same visible section of the screen that my input box was in. There are two reasons why this is important.

First, if there is some kind of a change on the screen, you want visitors to notice it. But if the change happens "off screen," folks might not notice that the change has actually occurred and they will continue to resubmit information in frustration. This is, of course, closely related to some of the feedback issues I mentioned earlier, but in this case, the feedback *is* taking place, just not where it's visible. ("Trees falling in the forest . . .")

Second, even with a scroll-friendly page, we don't want folks to have to scroll more than necessary. It is incredibly irritating to have to scroll a tiny bit just to click a Submit button that's barely outside the visible range of the screen. As screens get smaller, we can infer that more and more buttons, input boxes, and output boxes are going to have to be repeated, perhaps at the top *and* bottom of a page, which is an ergonomic consideration that is closely related to the placement of barcodes on aircraft boarding cards that I mentioned in Chapter 3.

Scrolling, menu length, and mobile phones

Although scrolling on smartphones is pretty straightforward, on less expensive models, people still have to use a physical button of some kind to scroll down a list of choices. When it comes to visibility, it's not always easy to see if there's more to a list than meets the eye.

Some mobile phones, such as the Samsung Ultra Touch, only display a scrollbar when a menu screen is activated by touch or cursor button. If the screen is left alone for a while, the scrollbar disappears again. Even though the individual menu items are numbered, looking at the first screen sends out *no* visual signals that more menu items are available. Some Nokia phones solved this problem by making the last line a default More option plus a downward-pointing arrow.

So, the rule of thumb is this: If you expect people to scroll—for whatever reason—give them a solid visual clue! If the number of visible items in a small-screen menu is limited (as they almost always are) try to limit the total number of menu items in a particular category to the number you can display onscreen without scrolling. It's not that people *won't* scroll; they just need to know that they *have* to.

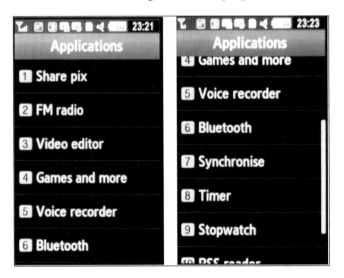

This Samsung phone has been kind enough to number the menu items. But the very first screen provides no clue as to how many items there are, nor does it display a visible scroll bar. The second screen provides better visual clues—if folks ever get to it. (Screen shots courtesy of Anders Schrøder)

Don't make important stuff look like an ad

In 1998, Jan Benway and David Lane from Rice University discovered an interesting phenomenon that they dubbed banner blindness. It seems people often missed the most important links on a page, particularly those within the top 60 pixels on a page where a banner ad might be. The previous year, Jared Spool et al. noticed that brightly colored, blinking stuff that looked like advertising was also ignored by users searching for content and functionality.

The irony of these findings is that the harder we work to make something visible, the more invisible it often becomes.

For quite some time, usability guru Jakob Nielsen included a video in his lectures of a usability test in which the test subject simply cannot spot a huge, red button that she needs to click even though it's in the middle of the screen. She looks at the main navigation. She clicks just about everything *except* the big, red button. Although we are tempted to laugh, this is really a sad commentary—and one that should remind us that if we do not empathize with our users, we will never design good products.

Over time, advertisers have developed various tricks to get us to click ads by making them look like content. And this works. So don't be surprised that the converse is true: If you want people to read and use your content, *don't* make it look like an ad, contextual navigation, or something else that suggests it will lead folks off in a completely new and completely unwanted direction.

USATODAY.com and banner blindness

USA Today, the colorful American daily newspaper, has long wrestled with issues related to banner blindness—and not always successfully.

I first became aware of the USATODAY.com redesigns in April 2000 at a conference in Boston. Here's the backstory as I remember it:

Sometime in the late 1990s, USATODAY.com learned through interviews and site statistics that most people were interested in three things: sports, weather, and stocks. So, naturally, the design solution was to put all three of these things right at the top of the web page in attractive, colorful boxes.

Guess what happened? No one clicked. Banner blindness.

A quick redesign later, and after several years of tweaking, the next major move was to make the online newspaper more participatory and social-media friendly in March 2007. The top of the page yet again became a banner, encouraging people to offer comments to articles—what they call "network journalism."[3] The main navigation for the page ended up being a tiny stripe along the left-hand side of the banner. To make things more confusing, a real banner ad, albeit thin, was inserted between the navigation header and the main content area.

In the communications industry, we sometimes refer to this kind of decision as knee-jerk design—a new buzzword comes along and everyone tries to get on the bandwagon. For *USA Today,* the term was network journalism.

At some point, USATODAY.com finally dropped the confusing non-banners and adopted a page header that is both attractive and seems highly functional.

---

[3] The term was coined by Buzzmachine founder and new-media proponent Jeff Jarvis.

The USATODAY.com site as it looked in the spring of 2007. The banner at the top was designed to encourage network journalism. Unfortunately, the main navigation is almost invisible, hiding as a thin column at the top left. Worse still, this header is completely cut off from the main content area by a FedEx ad!

After many years, it looks like USATODAY.com has finally acknowledged some basic usability best practices. This is the site as it appeared in February 2012.

Blocking out the sum

The sum total of a web-browsing experience has a huge effect on our desire to buy a product, continue with a service, or even sign up for something. Yet, we all know of websites where we can browse around to a limited extent only to hit some kind of a paywall when things really start to get good. Now, we must either register and surrender personal information, pony up some cash, or do something else to gain access to the really good stuff. It's kind of like the drug-dealer's business model when it comes to heroin addiction—the pusher gives folks junk for free to get them hooked. And I guess this approach also works in a lot of other situations given how often the technique is used.

One of the more curious experiences I've had recently was on Stumblehere.com. This is a classified-ad site; it's generally one of the better of its kind. However, on a recent visit I got a pop-up asking me to register for the site *each and every time I clicked*. Essentially, I was prevented from actually viewing the site (or "enjoying the customer journey" as we say in the user-experience biz). As a result, I didn't find what I was looking for, I didn't register, and I put this questionable series of events in a usability book. You've heard marketers talk about "win-win-win" situations? Well, this is "lose-lose-lose."

In the movie, *Jerry Maguire*, Jerry's potential client says, "Show me the money." In the usability biz, you've got to show folks value, too, if you want success. So, don't hide stuff, OK?

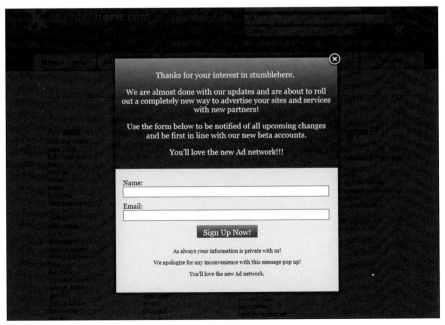

No matter what I did, each click on this website forced me to view this pop-up. The result was, I didn't find what I was looking for, I didn't register, and I put the story in a usability book. Definitely a "lose, lose, lose" situation for these folks.

These automatic doors at a home-improvement market aren't automatic at all. Worse still, the button to activate them (with your hands full of stuff) is so unrecognizable that an extra, handwritten sign is needed to show people where to poke (or kick, or elbow).

The check-in box on the British Airways site is at the top of the right-hand column. But many passengers search in vain through the choices offered directly in the main content area. Maybe *because* the check-in box is so prominent and has a different color, it becomes the victim of a kind of banner blindness, too.

Eric's Enlightening Elevator Examination

My favorite way to view the subject of visibility is to pretend that I just took an elevator up to a floor in an unfamiliar building. I step out and I need to know what to do next. Is the information I need visible? Are there signs or other hints as to where I should go? (In the old days, elevators had human operators. In department stores, they used to announce what was on each floor: "Second floor, ladies clothing, shoes, and lingerie . . .")

So, think of things this way, if you were operating that elevator (in real life or metaphorically as when taking your "passengers" to different web pages), what would you tell them? Whatever you have to say, make sure it's right there for everyone to see—as a clear headline, as a big sign, or anything else you think will help communicate things effectively. Architects talk about "wayfinding" when they do signage in the physical environment. But the principle is equally appropriate when it's applied to websites, restaurant menus, and a zillion other things. The key is visibility!

The primary reason folks come to this floor at the Zurich Airport is to use the restrooms. But the sign is located next to the elevator rather than across from it and can hardly be read due to the strong backlight. Hence, people exit the elevator and have no idea where to go.

The famous Berlin department store KaDeWe lets visitors know which floor they've arrived on when traveling on the escalator. A good solution, at least for folks going down. Going up makes things a bit less visible.

Sherlock, Edward, Don, and *Ch'i*

Somehow, it seems appropriate for a chapter that started with philosophical references to end the same way.

The Chinese system of geomancy, *feng shui*, suggests that clutter prevents the life-giving energy of the universe, *ch'i*, from flowing freely. And a million other folks have suggested that getting rid of irrelevant stuff makes the important stuff easier to spot. The great fictional detective Sherlock Holmes often remarked, "Eliminate the impossible, and whatever is left, however improbable, must be the truth." Designers are also detectives; they see the truth by eliminating the impossible (and irrelevant).

But as the noted American educator Edward Tufte has pointed out, when it comes to information, resorting to a reduction in the "resolution" of the information (by eliminating stuff or "dumbing down" explanations) is more indicative of poor design than of good design. And another highly respected designer, Don Norman, rails against those who demand simplicity: "We need complexity, even while we crave simplicity."

My point in bringing this up is that although we do want to keep stuff visible, we want to create designs that lead people to the most relevant choices without necessarily eliminating things that are relevant—even those things that are only occasionally so.

One of my favorite examples of this is the keyboard on concert grand pianos from the famed Austrian firm of Bösendorfer. More than a century ago, the Italian pianist Ferruccio Busoni asked the manufacturer to add extra bass keys to the standard keyboard so he could perform more accurate renditions of organ music (long organ pipes translate to long piano strings). Bösendorfer complied with both 92- and 97-key models in addition to the usual 88-key instruments. But a curious problem arose: The extra keys confused pianists. So, Bösendorfer disguised the extra keys so they didn't disturb the pianist's field of view. Rather than reducing complexity, Bösendorfer embraced it, and, quite literally, put it into proper perspective.

When we think about "visibility," we do need to think about Sherlock, Edward, Don, and our *ch'i*.

Most pianos have 88 keys, ending with A as the lowest note. This Bösendorfer concert grand features 92 keys with four extra notes going all the way down to a very low F. But because these extra keys distort the pianist's normal sitting position vis-à-vis the center of the instrument and fool with the artist's peripheral vision, Bösendorfer has made the two extra white keys black, which is a curious case of making the visible *in*visible to improve usability.

▶ THE "PERKS" OF BUSINESS TRAVEL
A TALE FROM THE TRENCHES

OUR OFFICE IN BUDAPEST invited me to speak at a conference and put me up at the rather posh Sofitel. What's more, they pulled some strings and got me a room over-looking the Danube River and Budapest's famous Chain Bridge. It was marvelous.

The room was certainly well-equipped, including a brand-new Nespresso coffee-maker. As I love a good strong cup of coffee to kick-start the day, this was a welcome feature.

My talk went very well. Naturally, there were the obligatory drinks and dinner after-wards, and I did my best to fulfill my social responsibilities. Alas, I had an early flight out the next morning, so as the evening wore on, the Nespresso machine back in my room looked better and better.

The next morning, I greeted the dawn and stumbled over to the coffee maker. I plunked in a coffee capsule, punched the start button and . . . oops. It didn't work. Or it was unplugged. Or something. At any rate, there were no little red lights, bubbling sounds, or other indications that my perk was perking.

I turned on and off every electrical switch I could find. The more desperate I became, the greater the Stoic calm exhibited by the Nespresso machine. With an effort far greater than I was really prepared to make at 5:30 in the morning, I moved the dresser from the wall to check the plugs. In doing so, I knocked over one of those countless lit-tle signs that hotels love to clutter desks with: "If you find out that the tea kettle does not switch on, please use the switch beside your bed."

OK. Er . . . why do you need a separate switch for these machines? Oh well. I actually don't give a damn. I just want to find this switch so I can get my coffee, pack, and catch my plane.

I wiggled everything electrical on the other side of the room, but to no avail. I even moved the bed. Only then did I notice two small brass switches built into the head-board. As both featured small "bell" icons, I assumed they would call a chamber-maid; they looked rather like the call buttons to the nurse's station at a hospital. But caffeine-deprived as I was, I finally decided to click one of them, even if it meant giving an apology and a tip to some sleepy housekeeper. Amazingly, the Nespresso machine blinked, burped, and burbled. And my day took a definite turn for the better.

THE "PERKS" OF BUSINESS TRAVEL
A TALE FROM THE TRENCHES

The lesson to be learned here is this: The more unfamiliar the surroundings, the more things need to be in plain view if you expect people to use them. Visibility, folks, visibility!

A first-rate coffee-maker and an electric tea kettle are provided in rooms at the Sofitel in Budapest, Hungary. Ah, Nespresso—the perfect way to start a new day . . . particularly after a long evening.

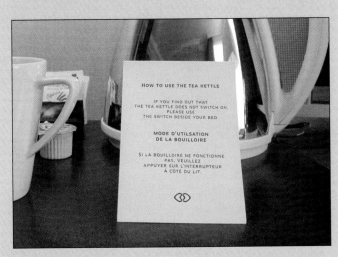

HOW TO USE THE TEA KETTLE

IF YOU FIND OUT THAT
THE TEA KETTLE DOES NOT SWITCH ON,
PLEASE USE
THE SWITCH BESIDE YOUR BED.

MODE D'UTILSATION
DE LA BOUILLOIRE

SI LA BOUILLOIRE NE FONCTIONNE
PAS, VEUILLEZ
APPUYER SUR L'INTERRUPTEUR
À CÔTÉ DU LIT.

Oops. After 10 minutes of trying to get the coffee machine to turn on, I finally spotted this note next to the tea kettle. It took several more minutes to locate the real switch, which was next to the bed.

MORE >

THE "PERKS" OF BUSINESS TRAVEL
A TALE FROM THE TRENCHES

These small buttons are built into the headboard of the bed. Although they didn't look like the other electrical switches in the room, they did turn on the coffee machine. I ignored them at first because they featured a bell symbol—I assumed they called the maid. Not the most visible or logical solution.

TEN INVISIBLE THINGS TO LOOK FOR

1. Does your stuff suggest that information is available when it really isn't? Or you've hidden it somewhere folks aren't looking?

2. Is something physically blocking the view to your information? Pop-ups? Physical hindrances? Something else? Get rid of these!

3. Does important information look like junk to be ignored, such as a banner ad or something else of questionable relevance?

4. Did you simply forget to include important information that people need in order to complete a task of some kind?

5. Does your stuff feature a "fold"? If so, is information grouped so things the user needs simultaneously are all on the same side of the fold? Or does the fold separate name and address, input and output, cookies and milk? Or is important stuff, such as a key contact link, hidden below the fold?

6. Are your long onscreen pages sending out a strong signal that you expect folks to scroll?

7. Is your paywall getting in the way of the free part of the experience?

8. Can every page on your website, every door in your building, every new view and vista of your stuff meet the demands of Eric's Enlightening Elevator Examination?

9. Is your design team reducing clutter because it makes stuff better or because it just makes things prettier? Better is better.

10. Are you using internal or proprietary branded terms instead of generic words that help people accomplish a task? For example, do you say "sign up for our Total Flexibility Plan" instead of "buy insurance"?

OTHER BOOKS YOU MIGHT LIKE

I admit that the six books I list here represent a real hodge-podge of topics. But I love them all and they all relate to visibility in one way or another, although some are related in a fairly obscure way.

- *The Image of the City*, Kevin Lynch, MIT Press, 1960
- *Wayshowing*, Per Mollerup, Lars Müller Publishers, 2005
- *Ambient Findability*, Peter Morville, O'Reilly, 2005
- *Handheld Usability*, Scott Weiss, John Wiley & Sons, 2002
- *Visual Explanations*, Edward R. Tufte, Graphics Press, 1997
- *Designing for Small Screens*, Studio 7.5, Ava, 2005

THINGS TO GOOGLE

- Banner blindness
- Mobile menus
- The myth of the fold
- Advertising on the web
- Wayfinding
- Eyetracking
- Newspaper design

Chapter Seven

Understandable

The English language has an incredible number of phrases that essentially mean the same thing:

- ▶ Get my drift?
- ▶ Did I make myself clear?
- ▶ Are you with the program?
- ▶ Are the dots connected?
- ▶ Are we talking the same language?

In usability terms, when it comes to "understandable," the answer to all of these colloquial questions must be "yes." If not, there is work to be done!

Let's assume that for any given thing, the engineer knows how to work the knobs and buttons, the designer knows what all the icons mean, the waiter knows that a particular dish is going to take 30 minutes to make. But if I don't have a shared frame of reference with these folks, usability is going to suffer: I'll push the wrong buttons; I'll click around aimlessly; I'll get mad because my meal is taking longer than I expected.

The concept of "shared reference" is really the *only* point I have to make in this chapter. On the other hand, it's incredibly important. Moreover, if you start to look at things in terms of shared reference, you'll find you can avoid an incredible number of dumb usability problems. Who knows—you might also see some of the earlier chapters in a slightly new light, too!

My Dad was an Austrian Jew who managed to escape his homeland in 1939. Here's a copy of the annexation referendum of March 13, 1938—which leaves no doubt as to what was expected from voters—one of the more scary examples of shared-reference building.

What is "shared reference"?

In the most basic terms, shared reference means that whoever is using something shares the same basic understanding of it as those who made it. Are we all on the same page? I hope so!

When it comes to interactive media, you have three tools at your disposal:

▶ Words

▶ Images

▶ Sounds

Everywhere else, all five of your senses helps establish shared references as you navigate your daily lives. Let's take a look at how this plays out.

A word about words

No matter how fancy things get in terms of graphics, no matter how intuitive we may think something is, words continue to play an incredibly important role in helping us understand the world around us. This is why books generally have more words than pictures. It's why even the cool icons on your iPhone have words associated with them. And words form the backbone of most instructional manuals, menus, product descriptions, marketing materials, PR, and so on. The ability to use words is so important that literacy rates are considered a key indicator of a country's developmental rank.

In usability terms, there are just two things to remember:

▶ Whatever you say, say it clearly.

▶ Don't assume everyone reads as well as you write.

Number of file	1 ▾	
File attach		Browse...

We may send information on offers and promotion in conjunction with our business partners.
Please check this box if you do not want to receive this?
Yes, keep me informed of the latest news on Samsung products, special offers, contests
with fabulous prizes, and events. ☐

+ Send	+ Reset	+ Close

This is an old screen shot from 2005. What do *you* think is going to happen if you check the box?
It took Samsung about a year to spot this goofy error. (Screen capture courtesy of Mark Hurst)

Eric's "light bulb" test

Years ago, when I started teaching "writing for the web," I developed a little game. I raised my hand, holding an imaginary lightbulb. I then told the folks in the room what I was holding:

> "I have in my hand an ordinary 60W light bulb with a standard E27, screw-in base. 'E27' means 'Edison 27 millimeter' which was Edison's standard fitting system for electrical connectors, which he introduced in 1909. OK. So, I have this ordinary 60W light bulb. Do you all know what I have in my hand?"

Over the past 15 years, I have played this game hundreds of times for thousands of people. Not once has anyone said that they *didn't* know what I was holding.

I then hold up a white, frosted incandescent light bulb and ask if this is what people thought I had been holding. And everyone agrees that this is indeed the bulb I described. But I tricked them.

By adding all of the irrelevant historical stuff about the E27 base, I get them to forget that they should probably be focusing on completely different details—most of which I have neglected to include in my description. In other words, I sucker-punched the audience.

While playing the game, I pass out small bags, each of which contains a light bulb. After I hold up a real bulb (white, frosted), I ask those who are holding bags to tell me if what they have in their bag is the same as my bulb. And none of these bulbs are, even though each and every one of them meets my description.

Here are some of the questions that point out details I "forgot" to put in my description:

▶ Is the bulb clear, colored, or frosted?

▶ Is it a special "daylight" bulb with a specific color temperature?

▶ Is it a special bulb for a darkroom?

▶ Is it a UV light to detect phosphorescent materials?

▶ Is it an energy-reducing fluorescent bulb?

▶ Is it 110V or 220V?

▶ Is it burned out?

Now at this point, you're probably thinking, "Well, Reiss certainly has weird ideas as to what 'ordinary' is . . . a darkroom bulb? C'mon, who's he kidding?" And that is *precisely* the problem. Ordinary can mean so many different things—there is no shared reference!

For those of you who are actually writing copy for websites, catalogs, brochures, instruction booklets, and so on, here's another important lesson to be learned: Don't get so wrapped up in describing a detail (or even a unique, competition-crushing feature) that you forget to include basic descriptive information. This is a horrifyingly common mistake.

All these bulbs are 60W units with a standard E27 base. But in fact, no two of them are alike. I'm constantly amazed by how much copywriters take for granted that we readers already know when they write content for catalogs and websites.

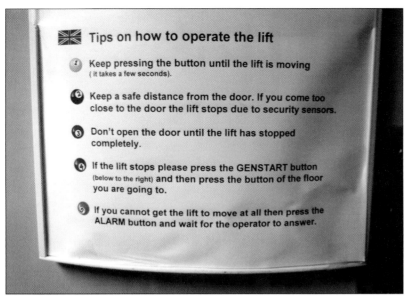

Here's a Danish elevator that actually needed instructions. The shared reference is established (in several languages), but the fundamental usability problem has not been addressed.

Five keys to creating effective "shared references"

This is the list I give my "Writing for the Web" students:

- ▶ Don't take anything for granted.
- ▶ Anticipate the questions people might have.
- ▶ Answer questions they didn't think to ask.
- ▶ Examine content in the context of your visitor's situation.
- ▶ The communication environment—the time and place surrounding an experience—will affect the nature of the information needed (or provided) at any given time.

Let me review these very quickly.

First, assume that people just don't have the same level of knowledge (or even interest) in what you are describing. So make sure to flesh everything out—including the obvious details. Repeating the obvious is reassuring to potential buyers of your products and services—or even your ideas.

Here's a tip: Read a description aloud and then have your friends ask questions. This exercise tells you a lot about information that you might have neglected to include. For example, anything they ask you that cannot be answered by reading a description (or looking at a photo) means something is missing and your shared reference has not been satisfactorily created.

If you look at information within the context of a scenario/story/situation of some kind, you can find lots of ways to improve the shared reference. Online, this probably means more descriptive text and better graphics. Offline, it often entails observing or imagining a specific user situation. Here's an example:

Let's say you and your partner plan to dine at a restaurant you haven't visited before. Here's a quick look at some of the touchpoints along your customer journey—all of which relate directly to the presence or absence of a shared reference. For example, if you made a reservation online, could you easily fill out the form? How quickly did you get a confirmation? Or did you call? If so, how did you find the phone number? How did you get to the restaurant? Did you drive, walk, ride with others, or take a taxi? Was the address easy to find? Was someone ready to seat you? Or was there a sign that says "Please wait. Our hostess will seat you shortly." Or were you left to your own devices? Did your server bring the menu promptly? Was it easy to read? Was there enough light to read it? Was it understandable or did the chef use fancy cooking terms you'd never heard before[1]. What about portion size? Did you order a starter? If so, did the starter end up being a meal in itself? Did you have to quiz your server or could you trust the menu descriptions?

Even with a simple scenario there are a lot of things to consider. There are shared-reference issues. There are service-design issues. There are wayfinding issues. There are architectural issues. And there are lots of chances to optimize usability—in the broadest sense of the word.

This leads directly to the last point on my list: the communications environment. Obviously, if you are checking out a restaurant online, you won't be getting the same sensory feedback you would at the restaurant itself ("Ooh. Look what they're having at the next table. I'd like that, too."). In other words, the experience that provides the information necessary to establish a shared reference almost always depends on where that experience is taking place.

Whenever you see extra signs stuck on common objects or interfaces, you can be sure that there is a basic design problem that needs solving. Here, a pair of door handles has failed to send a strong cognitive signal to users.

[1]This is from a fake menu written by a wonderfully wacky Australian foodie, Paul Raphael: "Twice-fingered Harris Ranch Wagyu beef, prepared sous vide in tepid water, garlanded with imported thistle and served in an unfired clay pot."

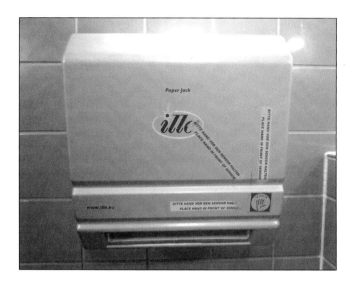

The "automatic" function of this hand drier was apparently so non-intuitive that *three* extra stickers were needed to explain to folks what they should do.

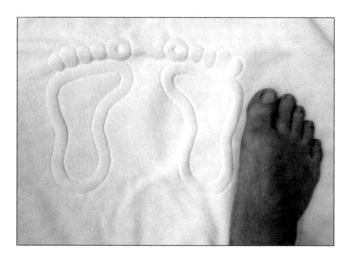

This bathmat at a Moscow hotel sends out clear signals that it's a bathmat and not a towel. Very nice shared-reference building in an unexpected place!

Creating a comfort zone

Earlier, I mentioned that travel is always interesting because it highlights so many usability problems. I am often outside my comfort zone in terms of understanding what I am expected to do. And like a traveler, visitors to your place of business—on- or offline—might also be outside their comfort zones. So, make them feel welcome. Take them by the hand. Provide the guidance they need to reach their goals and stay out of trouble.

Did you know that tourists flock to McDonald's in exciting cities such as Rome and Paris—cities that are famous for providing more sophisticated culinary experiences than a Big Mac®? It's because McDonald's has been supremely good about creating comfort zones for people who need a break from the stress of dealing with unfamiliar routines. No matter where you are, ordering at a McDonald's is pretty much the same from Sheboygan to Shanghai—which is the secret behind many successful franchises.

Don't be afraid to tell your story

There are perhaps the three most dangerous myths in online design.

► "Oh, our customers already know this. We don't need to say it again."

► "Web text should be no longer than 10 lines."

► "People don't scroll on the web."

The first is the reason so many opportunities to create a strong shared reference are missed—such as neglecting to say if a bulb is 110V or 220V, or if local sales tax is included in the price.

The second remark was made by usability guru Jakob Nielsen back in the mid-nineties when pokey computers were downloading verbose text over pokey dial-up modems. Back then, it was good advice. Today, it is absurdly out-of-date. Yet information lives forever on the Internet—for better and for worse—even though times change pretty fast in cyberspace. But don't just take my word for it: In 2004, `Marketingexperiments.com` showed that long text outperformed short text by more than 40 percent!

The third remark has been disproved countless times. In fact, the average Amazon book page is about 14 printed pages. Clearly, people *do* scroll—and a report from Razorfish in 2008 showed that almost 75 percent of people scroll before they do anything else! They scan and skim a page and only then zero in on something they read in detail. They look for keywords (nouns) and trigger words (adjectives) that relate to whatever it is they want to find out about—"non-iron shirt" for example, "non-iron" being the trigger and "shirt" being the keyword.

Curiously, the King of Hearts' in Lewis Carroll's *Alice's Adventures in Wonderland* accurately defined the proper length for web text: "Begin at the beginning and go on till you come to the end: then stop." In short, tell your story in a simple, straightforward way. Fill in the blanks. Don't leave out the details. Build the comfort zone that surrounds a solid shared reference.

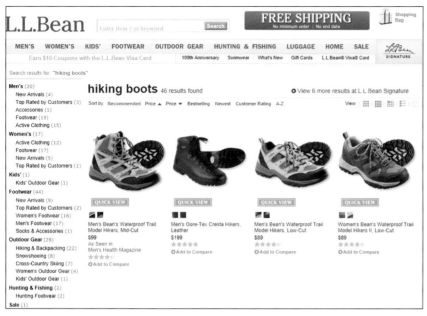

LL Bean is very good about creating shared references. Here, they've flipped the shoes so would-be hikers can see the sole—a key feature of boots like these.

Of course, Sears, Roebuck & Co. understood the importance of creating shared references more than 100 years ago. Here's a typical shoe page from its 1897 catalog.

This cryptic ad was on the back of a Copenhagen bus. "530g"—is that heavy or light? I went home and weighed my big clunky wing-tips, which were only 491g. Years later, I learned that this was a steel-toed safety boot, and a lightweight one at that! Finally, a shared reference.

Photos and other visual aids

Sometimes a picture really *is* worth a thousand words. An image can help improve the "scent" of your words. Most importantly, an image can flesh out stories that are difficult to tell using words alone. For example, I cannot imagine a future bride picking out a wedding dress on the basis of a description alone. Words are great for communicating facts and figures. But photos, graphics and other images are often better at conveying the subtle, often emotional aspects of an object. And if special functionality is involved, well, sometimes a picture *is* worth 1000 words.

Imagine, if you will, a tiny, hand-held camcorder that "easily fits in a pocket or purse." Well, how big a pocket? How big a purse? A photo of the device that is actually being held in a hand would be very useful indeed. In this instance, the hand is providing a frame of reference regarding the size of the unit. In general, including objects of a known size can help people understand the size of an unfamiliar object.

In other instances, a photo can demonstrate how something can be used, worn, and so on. This is particularly helpful if a product is to be used in a slightly unusual way, such as a vacuum cleaner that is worn on the back.

Finally, please remember that pictures and images alone are probably not enough to tell your whole story. Don't be afraid to use more than one shared-reference technique to get your message across.

Not only does the photo show how this clever vacuum cleaner is used (great for stairs or when cleaning crowded public spaces), it also gives an indication of the size. Detailed product specs are further down the page. All in all, great shared-reference building!

In Berlin, GPS data is used to predict when a bus will arrive, creating a great shared reference for those waiting at a cold bus stop in the middle of the night.

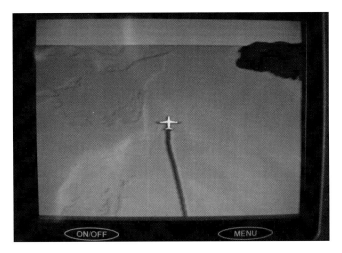

Scandinavian Airlines decided to get fancy with its in-flight map and show the view from the pilot's seat. Cute, but not very helpful. For example, did you figure out that the brown lump off to the right was actually Greenland?

Icons and other troublemakers

In 1997, I was working at an ad agency. The largest single item on any website budget was for designing the icons. Not content. Not navigation. Not structure. But icons. Somehow, we thought that the fewer words, the better. Keep in mind, this was a very new medium for all of us, so we were making up a lot of stuff as we went along.

Over the past 15 years, we've learned that icons, while attractive, are actually pretty poor communicators. In fact, there are only four icons that stand a decent chance of being recognized by most people:

▶ Magnifying glass (search)

▶ House (home)

▶ Envelope (contact/mail)

▶ Printer (print)

That said, I've heard people during usability tests look at the envelope and think it was a toolbox, a delete button, and lots of other stuff. Icons are pretty tricky.

Although it goes against the grain of any good designer, the chances are that if you really need an icon, you're better off using something similar to designs from Microsoft, Apple, or Google. Remember, people learn things on a site or app and expect to be able to use this knowledge on other sites and apps, too.

Therefore, I beg you not to get too creative when it comes to icons. They are pretty, but they are expensive to design. And the really creative icons generally make sense only *after* they've been clicked on—which somewhat defeats their main purpose! Remember that the *concept* of anything online is what it can *do*, not how it *looks*. Put your money where it counts: in meaningful content. Only when your content is in place should you be worrying about icons and other eye-candy.

This screen for the Danish Illy website is from June 1998, back when we thought icons were more important than words. Can you guess the purpose of the lower icon on the left? Will it help if I told you it's a Danish light switch? What if I told you that a switch, in Danish is called a "kontakt"?

"As big as a breadbox"

A couple of years ago, I was given an actual breadbox. To be frank, I've never really wanted one, nor did I see the point in wasting valuable counter space in my kitchen. But I was familiar with the traditional shared-reference question, "Is it bigger than a breadbox?" So what did I do? I spent the weekend trying to see what I could stuff into a breadbox. I think the oddest item was a small inflatable pool for my granddaughter. Technically, that makes a child's swimming pool smaller than a breadbox[2].

But here's my point: using something else as a point of reference—"as big as a breadbox . . . thin as an eggshell . . . tastes like chicken . . ." requires that the second reference is understood and makes sense. Often it isn't.

Let's take "chicken." What *did* I mean when I wrote, "tastes like chicken"? "Pollo asado" in Havana, Cuba? Or Kentucky Fried in Havana, Illinois? Our shared-reference recipe would benefit

---

[2]No animals were harmed in the making of this book—although my curiosity did scare the crap out of Gus the Cat when I tried to coax him into the breadbox, too. All electronic files are made from 100 percent recycled electrons.

from a pinch of geography. And if you haven't tasted "pollo asado a lo cubano" then my reference is meaningless. As a communicator, it is *my* responsibility to create a true shared reference, not to build a state of fear, uncertainty, or doubt in the minds of those receiving my message.

Classic – A669.30008.11SBO			
In 1986 Mondaine converted the clock's legendary face and bold hands into wristwatch form. This one-of-a-kind, easily readable watch has become one of the true design classics recognized the world over. The straightforward and unadorned shape of the case and crystal make this watch a true time icon.	33.00	30 / 100 / 3	Quartz
Classic – A669.30008.16SBO			
In 1986 Mondaine converted the clock's legendary face and bold hands into wristwatch form. This one-of-a-kind, easily readable watch has become one of the true design classics recognized the world over. The straightforward and unadorned shape of the case and crystal make this watch a true time icon.	33.00	30 / 100 / 3	Quartz
Classic Gents brushed – A660.30314.16SBB			
In 1986 Mondaine converted the clock¿s legendary face and bold hands into wristwatch form. This one-of-a-kind, easily readable watch has become one of the true design classics recognized the world over. The straightforward and unadorned shape of the case and crystal make this watch a true time icon.	36.00	30 / 100 / 3	Quartz

I defy anyone to tell me the difference between the top two watches on the mondaine.ch website, makers of the official Swiss Railway Watch. Clearly, Mondaine knows something they're not sharing with the rest of us.

If you need a reference to something in terms of size, weight, color, taste, and smell, think through your comparisons very carefully. And think internationally. . . .

The sun never sets on the World Wide Web

Although I was born in Texas, I've spent most of my life in Europe. Texas and Europe are very different—which often comes as a surprise to Texans when they go abroad. My message to you is to keep in mind that people really do have different backgrounds, expectations, frames of reference, and much more. Whatever seems "right" or "standard" or a "no brainer" to you, will invariably seem really strange to someone from another part of the country, continent, or hemisphere.

Here are some of the most frequent issues I've come across when dealing with communications—in print and on the web.

First name, last name is great for labeling forms—until you go to China, where the family name comes first. Actually, you don't even need to go to China—the Hungarians put the family name first, too. Can you see the problem? What *is* the "first" name? Just think of a basic contact form that requires you to type in your name in two boxes. "Family name" and "given name(s)" are perhaps better choices if you really intend to reach a wide audience (or are designing a multinational intranet where the employee directory is a key feature).

Units of measure are very tricky and often overlooked by content providers. If you mean inches, say so. If you mean centimeters, say so. Better yet, provide both measurements. And if you're operating with something slightly odd, such as British Thermal Units (BTU), make sure folks know which measurement—and even which abbreviation of the measurement—you are using. Curiously, most people understand the initials BTU much better than the official unit name.

Currency and taxes drive me crazy. If you need to give folks a price, let them know which currency you are using. Let them know if sales tax is included, too. Around the world, sales tax varies tremendously from city to city and country to country. For example, the City of Chicago currently adds about 10.5 percent, which makes this a pretty hefty "hidden cost" that first rears its expensive head at the cash register. This comes as a shock to Europeans who, although used to higher tax rates, usually see these taxes included in the advertised price. Make sure people understand your abbreviations, too; don't talk about VAT, MwSt, MOMS, HST, and so on without explaining what they mean. [3]

Most well-designed coins have a big number showing the value. A great help in establishing a shared reference for travelers unfamiliar with the local currency.

---

[3] VAT = Value Added Tax (United Kingdom). MwSt = Mehrvertsteuer (Germany). MOMS = Meromsætningsafgift (Denmark). HST = Harmonized Sales Tax (parts of Canada; actually Canada has three types of sales tax, including PST and GST. Google it—this footnote is out of space).

Suggestion Box

Your comments can help make our site better for everyone. If you've found something incorrect, broken, or frustrating on this page, let us know so that we can improve it. Please note that we are unable to respond directly to suggestions made via this form.

If you need help with an order, please contact Customer Service.

Please mark as many of the following boxes that apply:

☐ Product information is missing important details.
☐ Product information is incorrect. Propose corrections using our Online Catalog Update Form.
☐ The page contains typographical errors.
☐ The page takes too long to load.
☐ The page has a software bug in it.
☐ Content violates Amazon.com's policy on offensive language.
☐ Product offered violates Amazon.com's policy on items that can be listed for sale.

Comments or Examples:
Examples: Missing information such as dimensions and model number, typos, inaccuracies, etc.

[text area]

(Submit)

Years ago, I held a talk about shared references with folks from Amazon.com in the audience. They subsequently designed this simple suggestion box. A recent redesign did away with the box, but the principle remains and Amazon has created some of the strongest shared references in the online industry.

Audio and video

Greater bandwidth, a higher degree of format standardization, and the advent of easy-to-use third-party services, such as YouTube and Vimeo, make it possible to add true multimedia content to a website quickly and inexpensively. These are exceptionally useful shared-reference tools so use them!

Alas, there are various accessibility issues that are often used as an excuse for *not* using video and audio (blind people cannot see your video; deaf people cannot hear the audio). But if you set out to reduce everything to the lowest common denominator, you are going to be doing a lot of people a great disservice. If this is an issue in your politically correct organization, take a careful look at the legislation. Please remember that being politically correct and staying legal *are not the same thing!*[4]

---

[4]In the United States, you need to look at the Americans with Disabilities Act, Paragraph 508 (often abbreviated ADA 508). Elsewhere, check out the recommendations from the World Wide Web Consortium (W3C). Note the use of the word "recommendations," not "requirements."

▶ FOR WHOM THE RINGTONE TOLLS
A TALE FROM THE TRENCHES

ONCE UPON A TIME, some guys in London were operating an online mobile phone portal. They called me for usability help. As their business was based on selling the physical products on their website, the whole notion of shared reference was important to them.

Them: "We want to increase our sales. What should we do?"

Me: "Well, right now, you're just repeating the factory phone descriptions. The more uncertain people feel about a product, the less likely they are to buy it. Your online product descriptions could be a lot better."

Them: "Fair enough, but who has time to actually investigate every single phone?"

Me: "Hmm. If you can't provide better descriptions yourself, what about getting users to provide reviews and recommendations?"

Them: "No. They might say bad things about a phone."

Me: "Would you rather they express their disappointment in the manufacturer rather than in your company? Isn't honesty a good policy?"

Them: (long pause) "We have some old stock we need to dump."

Me: (much longer pause) "Well, you could at least provide a full range of tech specs. For example, you don't mention if the phones are dual-band or tri-band."

Them: "All our phones are tri-band."

Me: "Actually, some of them aren't. And even if they were all tri-band, you don't say this anywhere on your site."

Them: "Listen, you're making this very difficult. We just want to sell more phones. Why are you asking all these bullsh*t questions? Can't you just change some colors or something."

We never got them as a client. I later learned the company had adopted the tagline: "We know *everything* about mobile phones. Just ask us!" Yet despite this brilliant marketing ploy, the company eventually went out of business. One small step for con-artists, one giant leap for consumers.

TEN QUESTIONS TO ASK—AND ANSWER

1.   How are your written descriptions? Are they accurate and comprehensive? Pick a page at random. Does it pass the "lightbulb" test? Try it on a family member or neighbor—someone who is *not* connected with your enterprise.

2.   Define three typical users of your products or services. Create a short story for each of them describing how they interact with your stuff across all channels. Can you see touchpoints that can be improved?

3.   Are you using abbreviations, company language, or difficult words that might not be understood by the folks who use your stuff? Can you eliminate this language or improve it?

4.   Can you find images that don't properly build the shared reference? Can you redo these images so they provide a better sense of size, function, and so on?

5.   Currency, sales tax, shipping charges, and even service charges at a restaurant—if you list prices, do people know what these include or don't include?

6.   Are there online pages or offline processes that are difficult to understand for folks outside your local or geographic area? Can you add a few words to make things more understandable?

7.   Do you have icons that do not have accompanying descriptive words? If so, add some, including alt attributes (those little yellow boxes that pop up when your mouse hovers over a word or image).

8.   Are there physical limitations from a visual design perspective that are preventing you from creating a full-blown shared reference? (For example, a text box that is too small to contain all the text it should). Is a redesign of certain elements possible?

9.   Are you making comparisons or creating analogies to help people understand your products and services? If so, do people understand these comparisons?

10. Is there anything in your written or visual descriptions that could actually mislead people? Assuming you're not out to cheat folks, what can you do to spin things in a more useful direction?

OTHER BOOKS YOU MIGHT LIKE

Here are a couple of books that I simply love. All of them deal with writing, but as this is such a key part of the shared-reference-building process, I wanted you to know about them.

- ▶ *Writing That Means Business*, Ellen Roddick, iUniverse, 2010
- ▶ *Web Word Wizardry*, Rachel McAlpine, Ten Speed Press, 2001
- ▶ *On Writing Well,* William Zinsser, Quill, 2001
- ▶ *Letting Go of the Words*, Ginny Redish, Morgan Kaufmann, 2007
- ▶ *Clout:the Art and Science of Influential Web Content*, Colleen Jones, New Riders, 2011

THINGS TO GOOGLE

- ▶ Shared references
- ▶ Cognitive dissonance
- ▶ 20 tips for writing for the web
- ▶ ADA 508
- ▶ Sales taxes in Canada (just to see how complicated this can get)

Chapter Eight

Logical

Remember the irritatingly left-brained "Mr. Spock" from *Star Trek*? I assure you, he's not usually the kind of person you want on a creative design team. Yet this chapter is all about being logical and rational. It's about using common sense and reason to figure something out—or help design something someone else needs to figure out. You actually *do* need to adopt a stern demeanor for a lot of what's going to follow. And be prepared to take some grief from your designer(s)—they're going to tell you that you are stifling their creativity. No, you're just making sure they continue to create elegantly clear solutions.

Three basic types of logical reasoning

Here's some background on how logical reasoning works that you might find helpful. Feel free to skip the next couple of paragraphs.

In very general terms, there are three types of reasoning:

Deductive reasoning is how we arrive at the "truth"—whatever that may be. It means that if A = B and B = C, then A = C. There is often something sequential about deductive reasoning, which I get to a little later in the chapter.

Inductive reasoning isn't necessarily true, but suggests the *probability* of something being true. It helps us make a judgment based on past observations: "Joe has been driving for 40 years. He has never had an accident and only one ticket. Therefore, Joe must be a good driver." What we don't know is how much driving Joe actually does. Maybe he walks or bikes most of the time. But the probability is high that Joe really *is* a good driver.

Retroductive inference is all about learning things in one situation and then applying these things in a new, but similar situation. Like understanding how to get around an unfamiliar airport: The plane is at the gate. The gate has a number and possibly a letter. Signs point the way. I talk more about this in the next two chapters in this section, "Consistent" and "Predictable."

All three of these ways of thinking about "stuff" affect our perceptions of "usability." Remember, when I say "stuff" I basically mean everything—physical objects, interactive objects, services, and so on. I hope you find this knowledge as useful as I have over the years.

The magic word—"why"

Remember, we don't want *other people* to think—we need to do the thinking for them, preferably ahead of time. But that also means any time someone uses the stuff you're making, if they ask themselves, "I wonder *why* they did that?" you know there's a usability problem.

Errors in logic are not always disastrous, but they're never good. Once again, you don't want to do anything to cause FUD—fear, uncertainty, or doubt.

If you skipped the first half of this book, I talked about five ease-of-use considerations:

▶ Functional (it actually works)

▶ Responsive (I know it's working; it knows where it's working)

▶ Ergonomic (I can easily see, click, poke, twist, and turn stuff)

▶ Convenient (everything is right where I need it)

▶ Foolproof (the designer keeps me from making mistakes or breaking stuff)

Let's briefly revisit these, looking at them through the eyes of Mr. Spock (pointy ears are optional).

Functionality and logic

How often have you looked at the menu options on a computer screen and asked yourself, "Why aren't they letting me do that?" Probably a lot of times. Here are just some of the questions I've asked myself the past few days:

"Why won't the discount-ticket website let me add my frequent-flyer number? Why do I have to tell them at the airport?"

"Why is this miserable word-processing program bulleting the paragraphs above and below the text I carefully marked?"

"Why is my video projector so hot when it's on standby? Why is it using all this electricity when it's not in use?"

All these questions regarding functionality are completely logical within the given context.

Responsiveness and logic

"Why didn't" is the hallmark of most questions related to responsiveness issues. In all three of the following examples, it is logical to expect that the desired response would occur.

"Why didn't the elevator button light up when I pushed it?"

"Why didn't the hotel send me an e-mail confirmation?"

"Why didn't the receptionist answer the phone?"

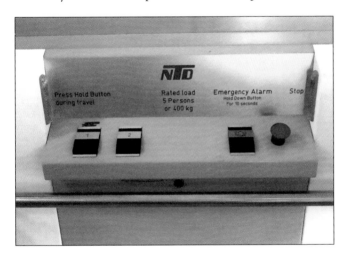

One assumes that the big, red button will stop this handicap elevator immediately. But why is it necessary to push the alarm button for 10 seconds? Is there really a greater chance people will accidentally push the alarm button than the "stop" button? I couldn't see the logic behind this design decision—particularly because people don't tend to read instructions during emergencies.

Ergonomics and logic

Back in Chapter Three, I discussed ergonomics. Good ergnonomic solutions also represent good common sense. Yet, time and time again, we are faced with silly usability problems that should have been caught by a good design team.

"Why is the cap on the shampoo impossible to unscrew when my hands are wet?"

"Why are the controls for the side mirrors on the car so far away that I cannot sit in a normal driving position while adjusting them?"

"Why do I have to scroll down to hit the Submit button after I've entered my username and password? Why isn't everything grouped?"

Anything here strike you as unreasonable? I'd say it's all pretty logical when you take the time to think about it.

The controls on this spa bath were difficult for me to understand—even close up and wearing glasses. Although the icons may have looked good on a designer's screen, why didn't anyone think about the specific communication environment?

Convenience and logic

Convenience and context go hand-in-hand. Yet how many times are our lives made more difficult because someone forgot this key point—from the layout of a grocery store to the layout of an interactive screen. Or something that should be a simple task-flow that somehow gets completely derailed.

"Why are the potato chips with the snacks, but the dip mix is with the salad dressings?"

"Why aren't the vacuum-cleaner bags listed on the same web page as the vacuums themselves?"

"Why can't I change the e-mail password on my smartphone without doing a full factory reset and losing all my data and apps?"

I bet you're already starting to make your own mental list of stuff that annoys you! And if you apply this kind of thinking to your own projects, you can probably nip a lot of usability issues in the bud.

This buffet at the Scandic Hotel in Copenhagen created problems for diners lined up on both sides of the service area: The forks were in the basket at the left, the knives were in the basket at the right. Why create confusion and irritation merely for the sake of symmetry? And why hide the knives and forks in baskets at all?

Foolproofing and logic

The questions here are all cries for help. That's why it follows logically that we, as designers should do just this—help those who are using our products and services before they get themselves into trouble.

"Why didn't the app remind me to save my data before it shut down?"

"Why aren't the instructions written so ordinary people can understand them?"

"Why did they let me do something this stupid?"

If you want to reach the ground floor in this elevator in Havana, Cuba, you have to push the Alarm button. The big sticker creates the shared reference, but why not just glue a "1" on the alarm button to solve the basic cognitive problem?

Design dissonance

Dissonance is a term taken from music. It means discord—something that is not in harmony. By design dissonance, I refer to stuff that sends out a cognitive signal of some kind that is actually at odds with the stuff's actual function.

Now sometimes, the results are merely amusing. For example, I once bought a cooking strainer on Bali that was made out of an old insecticide can. Somehow, the thought of putting something that had been in contact with poison in the food I was preparing was very funny to me. There is no real usability problem here except for the potential bad PR your product may suffer.

But on other occasions, the results can be very misleading. For example, my wife brought home some green-tea bath salts with a drawing of a woman drinking tea on the packet. To negate this silly design decision, the manufacturer also printed a big warning on the front telling folks that this was *not* something you could drink. This is classic design dissonance that defies all common logic; the designers created a problem that has the potential to make someone very, very sick. This situation would have been easy to avoid by simply changing the visual.

The takeaway here is simple: your design needs to support the mental model folks already may have. You don't want their experience with your stuff to start with a push in the wrong direction.

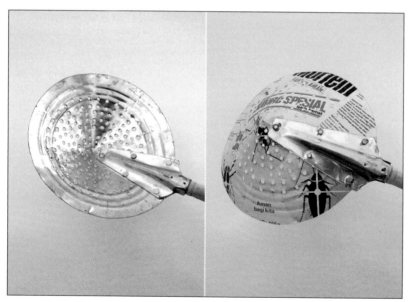

This food strainer from Bali is made from an old can of insect poison. A pragmatic solution? Certainly. But also a great example of design dissonance.

The illustration on this packet of Japanese bath salts suggests that it contains green tea to drink. Hence the disclaimer at the bottom: "!NOT FOOD!" If you want to create a shared reference, why start by pointing folks in the wrong direction?

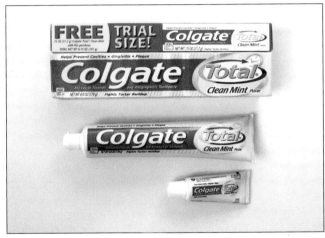

Even though "Free trial size" is clearly marked at the top of the double box, the relative sizes of the actual tubes are very different. Why take the chance of disappointing a customer through misleading packaging?

Once upon a time, these little trees were green and smelled of pine needles. Somehow, a blue "tree" that smells of "new car" strikes me as somewhat odd. I share this here because it's one of those rare instances where design dissonance *doesn't* affect usability.

Use cases

In Chapter 7, I spoke briefly about user scenarios, which are usually narrative stories, probably linked to one or more of the personas I mentioned in Chapter 4. Now, let's take a quick look at a third tool: use cases.

Use cases are schematic diagrams that show how various tasks are completed using boxes and arrows to show the flow. These often grow out of the needs identified in a scenario—sometimes you also hear it called a "user story."

The Pareto Principle[1]—80 percent of the actions come from 20 percent of the causes—also applies here; about 20 percent of your possible use cases account for about 80 percent of what happens with your stuff—particularly the online stuff. Those very basic cases that represent the 20 percent of the causes, are often termed "sunny day cases" or "happy paths." The edge cases (and there will be many) that represent 80 percent of the causes, but only apply to 20 percent of the actions are, not surprisingly, called "rainy day cases."

If you take a typical social-media site, such as Twitter, "creating an account" is clearly a sunny day case. So is "changing a password." But "identifying individual authorship in multi-user corporate accounts" is one of those rainy day cases—so much so that Twitter hasn't yet addressed this.

Here's how you can put simple use cases to work for yourself. Write a list of what you consider to be the key sunny day cases. After you've identified these, give them individual names, and start mapping out the flow:

"Case 1, Make tea. Enter kitchen. Go to stove and get kettle. Go to sink. Fill kettle with water. Put kettle on stove. Turn on burner. Get teapot. . . ."

You can also make a much simpler flow where you only chart out the very basic interactions, but don't go into the same level of detail. What you choose to do depends entirely on what kind of clarification you need. Typically, use cases can be created on any of three basic levels:

▶ General flows showing basic workflow but few details

▶ Touchpoint and service-design flows that show many interactions

▶ Flow schematics that can be used to program a routine

If you map out the flow of an existing routine, such as a shopping cart or booking engine, you may well spot procedures that strike you as odd. If so, you've probably found something that is causing usability problems because it conflicts with the human deductive-reasoning process. Sometimes, these processes are slightly out of kilter because people aren't nearly as categorical when making decisions

---

[1]In 1906 Vilfredo Pareto, an Italian economist, noted that 80 percent of the land in Italy was owned by 20 percent of the people. Later, he observed that 20 percent of the pea pods in his garden contained 80 percent of the peas.

as computers are, but the computer dictated the design of the flow. Computers are very binary in their thinking. Black/white. On/off. Zero/one. People just aren't like this.

An example of a flow that is broken could be a shopping website that lets folks put things in a shopping cart without registering or logging in, and then "resets" the cart to "empty" when they finally do log in.

These use-case flows can get very detailed indeed, and it's not my aim to make you an expert. But even if you just scratch the surface of one of these flows, you'll undoubtedly find things you can improve. And if the technique really appeals to you, check out "Writing Effective Use Case and User Story Examples" on the GatherSpace.com website. It's a really nice, very straightforward review of the subject.

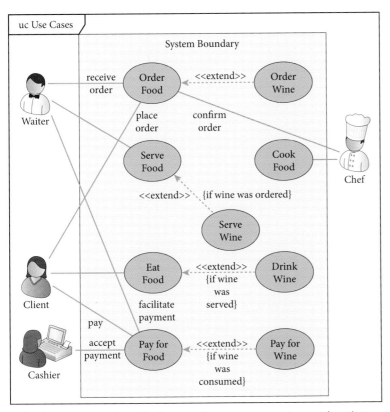

A simple use-case schematic diagram showing how a restaurant functions. (Author: Kishorekumar62, redrawn by Marcel Douwe Dekker. This file is licensed under the Creative Commons Attribution-Share Alike 3.0 Unported license)

Linear processes

The example of the "Make Tea" use case mentioned earlier also suggests that there is a certain linearity to many of these processes. After all, it makes less sense to get the teapot and find the tea before putting on the kettle. That's because we want to use the time waiting for the water to boil constructively. I suspect that the majority of logical problems relating to flows are linear in nature.

Over the years, I've come across

▶ Airline sites that forget to ask me to choose a seat until *after* I've printed my boarding card.

▶ Route-finder websites that ask me to choose a route *before* I've chosen my mode of transportation.

▶ E-commerce sites that first tell me they don't ship to my area *after* I'm halfway through the check-out.

▶ Restaurants that *wait* 20 minutes to tell me my chosen meal is not available that day.

▶ Software products that tell me to save my "single-use" activation key only *after* the shrink-wrap packaging on which it was printed has been thrown out.

The list is endless. But you can see how some simple changes in the linearity of the flow would easily set things right. "Highly logical," as Mr. Spock would say.

▶ SIX DETOURS ON THE ROAD TO USABLE NAVIGATION
A TALE FROM THE TRENCHES

IN THE SUMMER OF 2011, I rented a Cadillac CTS in Miami, FL. I had a lot of boxes to haul, so I wanted a big car, which automatically put me in the luxury car category. I wasn't about to complain—I like fancy cars. Moreover, as I would be driving to places beyond my normal stomping grounds, I was delighted to see it came with a built-in navigation system.

The Caddy's navigation screen magically rises out of the dashboard—if you know how to turn it on. Even though there are several specially marked buttons related to the navigation, I wasn't actually able to use the screen until I turned on the radio. Apparently, this rather odd (and for me illogical) set-up has become something of an industry standard as radios and navigation devices are now packaged together in integrated "infotainment" units. Serves me right for owning a 15-year-old car with stand-alone components.

When I finally figured out the on/off function, my next task was to enter some addresses. There was a surprising amount of typing involved, bad street-name suggestions, and other problems before I got things right—after which I promptly managed to delete my selection or did something else stupid. At any rate, I had to start the process again several times.

Now I'm sure a lot of you folks out there in Readerland have CTSs with navigation systems and you *love* yours. Well, to make up for some of my snark, let me share a discovery with you. Did you know that if you press three buttons simultaneously—FAV, INFO, and CONFIG—you get a bunch of secret extra features? Pretty cool, right? Pretty logical . . . er . . . well . . .

The next trick was to actually get the car to navigate from A to B. In one instance, A was south of Miami in Pinecrest, FL, and B was north in Fort Lauderdale. Now the first part of this journey should have been easy: Turn *left* out of the driveway, continue to the corner and turn right onto SW 67th Ave. But the navigation apparently wanted to show off. The digital monolog went something like this:

"Turn right onto SW 102nd St." (That should have been "left" but I'll play along.)

"Prepare to turn right." (. . . for the second time.)

MORE >

▶ SIX DETOURS ON THE ROAD TO USABLE NAVIGATION

A TALE FROM THE TRENCHES

"Turn right onto SW 64th Ave." (Ah. I see what you're up to.)

"Continue straight for ¼ mile."

"Prepare to turn right."

"Turn right onto SW 104 St." (OK. You're almost back on track.)

"Continue straight for ½ mile."

"Prepare to turn right."

"Turn right onto SW 67th Ave." (Finally, done with the sightseeing.)

So, instead of a simple turn out of the driveway, it sent me around the entire block. Big deal? Not if you're in unfamiliar territory. By the time I got to Fort Lauderdale, I was completely convinced that this car had never actually been to Florida before and was just making stuff up to amuse me. But hey, it's an infotainment system, right?

Honestly, the only truly logical part of my navigation experience was when the car got lost, and I stopped to ask directions at a gas station. And I bought a map.

TEN QUESTIONS TO ASK—AND ANSWER

1. As you review your project, are there any functional issues that make you stop and ask "Why did we do that?"

2. Are there responsiveness questions that also make you wonder why something is happening (or *not* happening)?

3. What about ergonomics? Are you being forced to scroll unnecessarily or need too many hands to accomplish something? Remember, if you ask "why," you could be on the track of something important.

4. Can you spot any situations related to convenience that cause you to ask yourself, "Why can't we make this easier?"

5. Did you make a mistake at some point? If so, can you think of a way to avoid the mistake? What about asking a family member, friend, or colleague to look at the same thing and see how they react?

6. Is there anything in your stuff that looks like one thing, but is actually something very different? Can you do something to reduce the design dissonance?

7. Try mapping out three or four sunny day use cases for your stuff. Now create a simple flow. Are there any things that seem unclear? Are the flows difficult to map out? If so, you might have spotted a key usability flaw.

8. What about the logic of the flow? Is each step on the way bringing you closer to the goal? Or are some flows taking you off on unnecessary tangents? If so, can you eliminate any of these detours?

9. Take a look at your stuff from the standpoint of shared-reference building (see Chapter 7). Are there places where better communication of an invisible process will help make things seem more logical to others?

10. As always, make sure the back button on the Internet browser does not "break" a routine that is already in progress.

OTHER BOOKS YOU MIGHT LIKE

Books on how we think can get pretty heavy duty. But these five are actually pretty entertaining. I hope you like them.

- *A Mind of Its Own: How Your Brain Distorts and Deceives*, Cordelia Fine, Icon, 2005

- *Predictably Irrational: The Hidden Forces That Shape Our Decisions*, Dan Ariely, HarperCollins, 2009

- *Irrationality*, Stuart Sutherland, Constable and Co., 1992

- *The Design of Everyday Things*, Donald A. Norman, Doubleday Business, 1990

- *Nudge*, Richard H. Thaler and Cass R. Sunstein, Penguin, 2009

THINGS TO GOOGLE

- Logic
- Pareto Principle
- Deductive reasoning
- Inductive reasoning
- Retroductive inference
- Design dissonance
- Use case example
- Use case diagram

Chapter Nine

Consistent

On any list of popular board games, *Monopoly* usually ranks close to the top. Even though the names of the individual property names may change in different versions, the basic layout of the board is pretty much the same, the relative values of individual properties remains the same, and the printed rules are also amazingly consistent, no matter who manufactured your particular set.

Consistency is one of the keys to achieving elegance and clarity in functional design. Remember, we're dealing with the psychological aspects of something—that it does what we *expect* it to do. Just as we expect our fellow *Monopoly* players to stick to the agreed rules (including any special "house rules" determined before the start of play). Only in reality TV shows do we find it amusing to see the rules suddenly change—to the despair of the celebrity wannabes involved.

Consistency makes our lives simpler by making the world around us a little easier to understand.

A caveat

The brilliant interface designer (and Apple Employee #66), Bruce Tognazzini once wrote, "Inconsistency: It is just important to be visually inconsistent when things must act differently as it is to be visually consistent when things act the same."

Please keep this important point in mind as you read this chapter.

Seduced by synonyms

Several words often mean the same thing—these are called synonyms in English. For example, car, auto, automobile, and vehicle all mean more or less the same thing. Synonyms are great for writers because they let us vary the language and make it more interesting. But on a website or on signage, using several different words at different times to give the same information can lead to serious problems.

For example, if you've been using Submit as a button label, don't suddenly change it to Send or Accept unless you want to confuse people. It also means that signage in a public facility needs to be standardized, too. For years, the Copenhagen Airport had had two different signs: Disabled Toilet and Handicap Toilet. The Disabled Toilet always raised a smile—"So when are they going to get around to fixing that broken toilet?"

In short, don't mix and match your terms just for the sake of creativity or out of sloppiness. After you have established your language conventions, stick to them, particularly where forms and dialog boxes are concerned.

That said, sometimes redundant links (links that appear on the same page and lead to the same place) can have slightly different wording. For example, a link in the header might read "Contact," whereas a text-embedded link might read, "If you have any questions, please don't hesitate to ask us." This is not necessarily bad because the two links are fairly similar. You run into problems, though, if the link reads "Light Bulbs," which is pretty specific but visitors land on a page titled "Spare Parts," which is much broader.

Keeping things homogeneous

Just as we want to keep our language standardized in terms of individual words, we also want to make the choices we give people easy and straightforward. For example, which of the following groups do you belong to?

- ▶ Men
- ▶ Women
- ▶ Children

Not too difficult, was it? This is a homogeneous list in that all the individual words (think of these as menu labels on a website) have clear distinctions with no overlap.

In Chapter Two I showed you some of the goofy choices that computer manufacturers give us online and explained how this causes fear, uncertainty, and doubt (FUD). These are typical of non-homogeneous lists, such as this one:

- ▶ Men
- ▶ Women
- ▶ People who wear glasses

Suddenly, the choice is a lot tougher. So, when designing usable choices—from menus on websites to menus in restaurants to signs in a grocery store—the key is to keep the choices as clear-cut and consistent as possible.

Here's the main page from the American online shoe retailer Zappos as it looked in early 2007. A lot of stuff going on here and a lot of non-homogeneous menus.

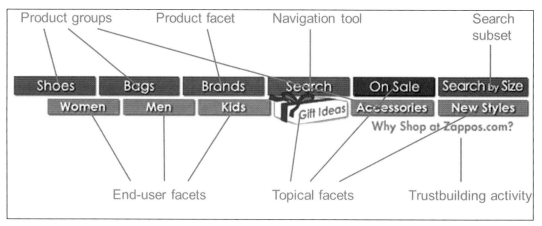

At first glance, the top navigation looks reasonable. But when you analyze it, you quickly find that it is kind of a mess.

But by late 2007 Zappos had started to clean things up. The second, big menu is item-based: "Flip Video, Eyewear, Handbags, Kids, Watches, Boots. . . ." Hang on a second! They sell "kids"? Can I buy a baby daughter? Does express delivery mean less than nine months?

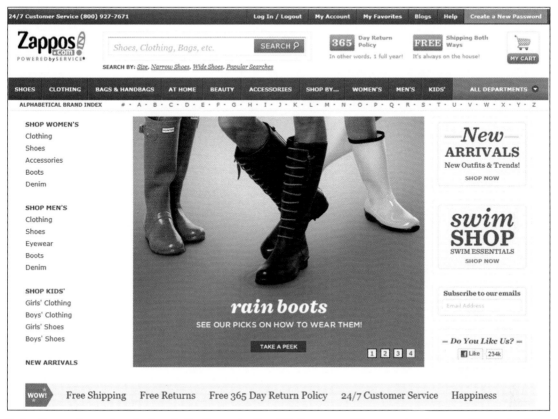

Today, Zappos has a clean look and effective navigation. OK, there are still some minor incongruities, but nothing that looks like it's going to create any serious problems. Well done folks!

Retroductive inference revisited

To recap from the last chapter, retroductive inference refers to the logical thought process where we apply things we've learned in one situation to a new, but similar, situation somewhere else. This is why most of us know how to order a meal in a restaurant, drive a borrowed car, buy a movie ticket, and behave well during meetings and at social occasions. Manners are an example of the things we learn when we're young and apply in many unfamiliar but related situations throughout our lives.

Our dependence on retroductive inference plays a huge role in how we experience usability. For example, seeing icons on a website that are similar to icons we have seen and used on other websites helps us understand what we are expected to do. However, if the icons on your site actually do something very different, visitors will be both surprised and frustrated.

In wayfinding and building signage, consistency is also critical if you expect people to get where they want to go quickly and efficiently. That said, building signage is one of those instances where each architect imparts his or her own design concepts, often with little regard for the work of others. And that brings us to standardization.

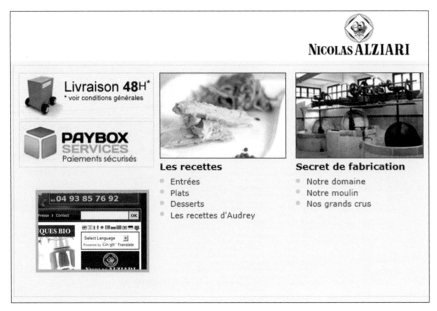

Nicholas Alziari of Nice, France produces some of the best olive oil in the world. But Google's automatic translation app, embedded in the site, is not doing the company any favors (see the inset box). The French site is written correctly. . . .

. . . but the English version (among others) gets way off track. "Recettes" (recipes) becomes "Revenues" and "Entrées" (starters) becomes "Inputs." Technically, these are correct translations, just not in this particular context. As a result, the experience of using this website is wildly inconsistent depending on the language being viewed.

Standardization promotes consistency

Sometime around 1915, car-rental companies began to spring up around the United States. Most of these operations centered on Henry Ford's iconic Model T. However, as popular as the Model T was, it was not an easy car to drive.

The accelerator (throttle) was actually a lever mounted on the right of the steering wheel column along with a second "timing" lever on the left that retarded or advanced the electrical spark to the plugs. There were three pedals: a shifter/clutch (used in conjunction with a floor-mounted lever), a brake, and a third pedal that put the car into reverse. There was no self-starter; you had to crank the car to turn the engine.

Henry's design remained more-or-less unchanged from 1908 until 1927. In the meantime, though, car controls had become much simpler. In fact, the 1916 Cadillac was the first car in the world to introduce the standard shift pattern we see in most modern vehicles.

These developments were followed closely by the car-rental companies because they didn't have time to give driving lessons to each new customer. And they pressured manufacturers, such as General Motors, to standardize a wide range of car controls. By the end of the 1920s, most cars operated pretty much the way standard-shift cars do today—including Ford's radically redesigned Model A, which he launched in May 1927. Moreover, Ford finally included a self-starter, possibly the last American manufacturer to adopt this feature.

Even in Internet years (like dog years), interaction design is still a young industry. We've probably moved beyond the Model T stage, but we're probably not as advanced as we like to think either.[1]

Today, the World Wide Web Consortium (W3C) seeks to define the technical standards needed to support interoperability, portability, and mobility. The International Standards Organization (ISO) helps define production, management, and service standards, (such as ISO 9000).

The point of standardization is not to put the brakes on creativity, but to build clarity into the solution.

Driving a Ford Model T would be difficult for most modern drivers. Here are the three foot pedals in a 1914 model: (from left to right) clutch/gear shift, reverse, and brake. The accelerator (throttle) is actually a lever on the steering wheel.

[1] I once worked out that an "Internet year" corresponds roughly to a single business cycle, or about 4.7 years. I have a blog post from September 2009 that talks about it. You can find it if you Google "Calculating the length of an internet year."

Throughout the 'teens and 20s, car-rental agencies pressured car manufacturers to standardize driving controls. Anyone today who can drive a stick shift would have little trouble starting and driving this 1931 Cadillac.

Don't take consistency for granted

You might think that "green" means "go" and "red" means "stop." But not always. For example, I have three chargers for camera batteries. When I start charging a battery, this is what I see:

▶ **Sony**: Red indicator light

▶ **Canon**: Yellow indicator light

▶ **Leica**: Green indicator light

When the battery is fully charged, the Leica and Sony lights go out, the Canon turns green. Now I realize that most of you don't have three digital cameras, but I bet you do have at least three digital devices that need recharging. And you've probably learned how to interpret all the signals without really having given much thought to the matter. But hey, if you are involved in designing stuff like this, it's worth a thought or two.

Have you given much thought to arrows on signs in public spaces? Most people don't. You'd be surprised at how little consistency there actually is. For example, an arrow that points up can mean straight ahead. But so can an arrow pointing down. This is confusing on signs where there are arrows pointing both up and down to indicate what happens on either side of the sign.

Look for these curious inconsistencies the next time you're walking around a shopping center, public park, train station, or airport.

There are lots of other things that aren't particularly consistent either—from door handles to thermostat controls. If you are out to establish a new convention, make sure you don't just invent a square wheel out of ego or ignorance.

In the late 1930s, the Royal Air Force in the United Kingdom defined what is now called the RAF "Basic Six" blind-flying controls and put them in standard positions in the center of the control panel. This made it significantly easier to train pilots on one aircraft and then switch them to another. Here's an illustration from the pilot's manual for the Spitfire MK VIII. (Crown copyright)

Barajas Airport in Madrid, Spain has arrows that point down . . .

. . . but Sheremetyevo Airport in Moscow, Russia has arrows that point up . . .

. . . .and Charles de Gaulle Airport in Paris, France can't make up its mind. Here are two signs, each using its own arrow convention.

This sign in Copenhagen says there is no parking between 3:00 p.m. and 6:00 p.m. At other times, one-hour parking is permitted on one side of the sign. But which side? Curiously, if you come across older signs, the arrow convention is reversed. After 35 years in the Danish capitol, I still get parking tickets.

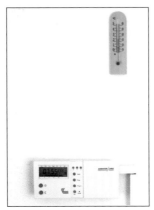

You'd think that something as ubiquitous as a thermostat would demonstrate a greater degree of consistency with current design practices. The read-out on this electronic thermostat in a Ukrainian hotel was so difficult for guests to decipher, the owner put up an old-fashioned thermometer, too.

One button, one function

Earlier in the book I mentioned the crazy VHS player I owned years ago—the one with 46 buttons on the front panel. Well, despite the many other usability problems with this unit, at least there were no multifunctional buttons. The truth is, if a single button is expected to do several different jobs, you are generally asking for trouble. People don't always understand that a machine or website is suddenly in a "different mode."

For example, on my TV, I can use the Menu button on the remote to activate the onscreen menu or turn it off. That's fine. I can figure that out. But there are also four cursor buttons that are used to navigate around the menu. The left-arrow button functions as a back button—unless the menu is off, in which case it flicks through 12 different screen aspect ratios (widescreen, movie expand 16:9, subtitle zoom, and so on). And if I press both the left and right arrows at the same time, I get a setup menu that is different from the menu I get when I press Menu. Once, I inadvertently turned all the menus into Finnish and had a terrible time straightening things out. (If you're having the same problem, look for "Kieli." You'll find it listed under "Asennus.")

Anyway, multifunctional buttons can be a real pain in the butt.

The Apple Corporation has been brilliant at both eliminating buttons and avoiding the multi-use problem. The iPhone only has one button and it only does one thing: bring you back to the front screen of the phone. Everything else is taken care of with so-called "soft" buttons that appear on the touchscreen. The Apple mouse only has one button (the first commercial mouse from Xerox had three buttons and was very confusing). That said, if you hold the Apple mouse button down for a couple of seconds, you get a second menu, much like the right button on a PC mouse. OK. It's a compromise, but it works and the behavior is easy to learn.

However, one button is not always simpler. And having more buttons is not always bad as long as they are grouped sensibly (to help communicate that these buttons probably represent related functions) and don't do different things at different times.

Consistency and simplicity always go hand-in-hand. But please don't confuse simplicity with ease-of-use, which isn't always the case.

This remote control for a TV satellite dish uses colors and physical layout to effectively group related functions. On the other hand, almost every button has more than one function; the combination Menu/Expand button is bound to cause trouble. All in all, it's not the worst design I've seen, but it's not the best either.

One icon, one function

Closely related to the discussion of buttons is the behavior of icons. For example, Google's popular Gmail application is notorious for reusing icons as is Google Docs. This is frustrating and confusing. After all, the whole purpose of icons is to provide a quick, cognitive hint as to what functionality lies behind.

Of course, Google isn't alone in this. Windows products, such as Outlook, also reuse icons. And Apple has been known to do so, too.

There isn't really much more to be said, except that clearly even the major players haven't really embraced the concept of "one icon, one function" as a best practice despite years of research and consumer complaints. More's the pity.

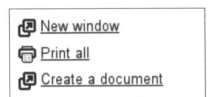

This box is from the now-discontinued Google Lab. It shows two identical icons, but serving different functions. By choosing one, folks could open a new window. By choosing the other, folks could create a Google Doc directly from Gmail; Apparently, the icons in this instance were merely for decorative purposes as they have good descriptive labels—without these labels, they would have been meaningless.

Here's a little sample of Google's Gmail in the fall of 2011 when the Google Lab app was activated. Suddenly, there are no visible words to help guide folks. Oops.

One object, one behavior

I have a constant fight with Microsoft Word. Some of the windows and pop-ups can be resized or repositioned by dragging various edges, but not all of them can. The lesson here is very simple: Make sure that objects that look alike also act alike.

This becomes even more important when there are so-called "invisible" functions on a page. Perhaps the most "visible" of these invisible functions are shortcut keys. Again, Microsoft Office programs are major culprits, particularly if you have different language versions installed on your home and office PC or if you switch from a PC to a Mac. In my case, some programs were in Danish and others were in English. And the shortcut keys were different—well, sort of.

For example, in MS Office 2010 for the PC, Ctrl+S saves a document in both the English and Danish versions of the program (Save = Gem in Danish). But Ctrl+I creates "italic" in English and "Indsæt hyperlink" (insert hyperlink) in Danish. So, why isn't the Danish version more consistent, for example by using Ctrl+G (for "gem") for the Save function? And to confuse things further, why do the same commands on a Danish Mac use *all* the English-language shortcuts?

Worse still is when programs, even when using the same language, change the function of a shortcut depending on where you are in the workflow. My advice? Make things consistent or expect people to complain.

▶ SPEED LIMIT SIGNS IN DENMARK— PUTTING BRAINS INTO TOP GEAR
A TALE FROM THE TRENCHES

IN A WORLD FULL of exceptional situations, happily, it's only the pedantic few who really insist on a policy of "no exceptions." Unhappily, one of these pedantic instances is the Danish Road Directorate, a division of the Ministry of Transport.

In Denmark, as in many other places around the world, speed limits are posted on round white signs with a red border. The speed limits themselves are standardized as follows:

- ▶ 50 km in cities
- ▶ 80 km on country roads
- ▶ 110 km on highways

Special signs appear if another speed limit is temporarily in effect. So far so good.

But here's where it gets tricky: Denmark has also adopted a second type of sign that is not often seen in other countries—a light gray version that tells drivers that the temporary speed limit has ended. Kind of like the End School Zone traffic signs you see in the United States.

The logic of this is fine: "Why do we need to advertise the standard speed limits? People are just supposed to know these. We will only mark the exceptions."

So, here I am, trying to keep my mind on the road and suddenly a sign tells me that a 70 kph speed limit has been lifted. And my brain is thrown into fifth gear. What did the sign mean? What should I do? Did I miss seeing another sign? Where is this road leading me? Am I approaching a town, which means reducing speed to 50 kph? Or can I speed up to 80 kph?

The really crazy thing is that putting up a sign that simply told me what the speed limit *is* rather than what it *isn't* wouldn't cost a penny more. Ah, but . . . "Drivers should *know* what the speed limit is. We shouldn't have to remind them."

Brilliant logic. Outstanding consistency. Crappy usability. This is the exception that proves the rule that all rules have exceptions.

SPEED LIMIT SIGNS IN DENMARK— PUTTING BRAINS INTO TOP GEAR
A TALE FROM THE TRENCHES

This typical European speed-limit sign tells drivers that 70 kilometers an hour is the legal maximum— an exception in relation to the standard speed limits in Denmark.

This gray sign only tells drivers that the temporary speed limit is no longer in effect. Why make drivers think? It would make more sense just to state the permissible limit. And it would be cheaper, too, because the department of roads wouldn't have to keep so many different signs in stock.

MORE >

▶ SPEED LIMIT SIGNS IN DENMARK— PUTTING BRAINS INTO TOP GEAR

A TALE FROM THE TRENCHES

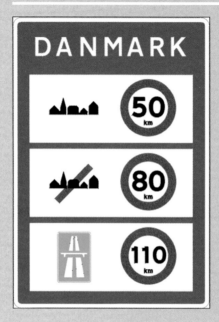

This is the official sign that welcomes drivers to Denmark. It is found at all borders and at the international airports, but nowhere else. Local drivers are simply supposed to know these things.

TEN QUESTIONS TO ASK—AND ANSWER

1. Are there any things in your design that look the same, but actually act differently? Make sure things that act different *look different*.

2. Are there things in your design that act the same but look different? Make sure that things that act the same *look the same*.

3. Is there anything in your stuff that seems different from similar stuff you've seen somewhere else? Is there some kind of design best practice that was overlooked or ignored?

4. Is the consistency of any object or function being sacrificed for the sake of creativity? What are these functions and objects? Can you see a quick fix that won't thoroughly offend the designers?

5. Do you have physical buttons and knobs and levers that are expected to do different things at different times? Would it make sense to add more buttons or levers?

6. Are there icons that are being reused for different functions? If so, either redesign the icons or get rid of them.

7. Can you increase the consistency of any objects or processes? Quite apart from adopting the best practices developed by others, try increasing functional uniformity within the context of your product or service.

8. Does your stuff require prior knowledge of similar products or services in order for folks to figure out how to use it? If so, will folks recognize this similarity when they encounter it? Make sure you give people strong visual clues that will trigger the knowledge they've picked up somewhere else.

9. Can you use colors and the physical grouping of buttons and other controls so that folks can immediately see that they are related in some way?

10. Has your stuff been "patched" at some point as a way to quickly fix an underlying consistency problem? If it's possible to actually fix things and eliminate the patch, maybe now is the time to do so. (See the photo of the Cuban elevator in Chapter Eight. It's a great example of a "patch.")

OTHER BOOKS YOU MIGHT LIKE

Surprisingly, less has been written on the subjects in this chapter than one might think, but here are some books that certainly touch on issues I've talked about here:

▶ *Living with Complexity*, Donald A. Norman, MIT Press, 2011

▶ *Simple and Usable*, Giles Colborne, New Riders, 2011

▶ *Everything is Miscellaneous: The Power of the New Digital Disorder*, David Weinberger, Time Books, 2007

THINGS TO GOOGLE

▶ Design consistency
▶ Multifunctional buttons
▶ One object one behavior
▶ Wayfinding
▶ Icon design
▶ How to drive a Model T
▶ Calculating the length of an Internet year

Chapter Ten

Predictable

For most people, predictability and consistency mean pretty much the same thing. Actually, I think there *is* a clear distinction: Consistent means something does the same thing each and every time; predictable means it does what you *expect* it to do. Let me give you a quick example.

In my house, all the electrical switches look alike and were approved by the same organization (Underwriter's Laboratories—UL). That's consistency. But when I travel somewhere I've never visited before, I expect to see switch-like objects next to doors that control the lights in a room—assuming there's electricity. That's predictability. The chances are really good these devices will either toggle in some manner or be a button that clicks on and off.[1]

As always, creating a proper shared reference lies at the heart of many predictability issues (see Chapter Seven). And retroductive inference also plays a huge role (see Chapters Eight and Nine—and stop skipping around).

---

[1] Of course, there's no guarantee that the switches are predictable as to either their function or location. See the "Tales from the Trenches" in Chapter Six. Or Google "Light switches - Mumbai, India" for a really funny article by "Steve." Check out his other articles, too. He has a lot of great anecdotes about usability as it applies to service design.

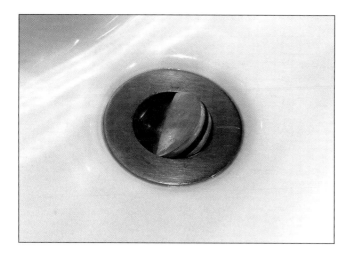

When closed, this sink stopper looks like it ought to be operated by a lever or handle somewhere near the faucet. Only when I poked at it in desperation did I find out that it pivoted in the middle. Talk about design dissonance. . . .

Black smoke from the Sistine Chapel means the conclave hasn't found a new pope (*fumata nera* = burn wet straw with the cardinals' used ballots); white smoke if a new pope has been elected (*fumata bianca* = burn the dry ballots alone). But when Benedict XVI was elected, the new, state-of-the-art chemicals produced a hard-to-see grey smoke. Oops.

Six ways to enhance predictability

We are creatures of habit. Change, while exciting, is also disruptive in many ways. This is perhaps why consistency and predictability are so often lumped together. Maybe this is also why consistency and predictability get so much grief from the creative crowd looking for "new and innovative" ways to do things.[2] In any event, here are some things I've discovered over the years that really help improve predictability:

- ▶ Let folks know what to expect before they get wherever they're going.
- ▶ Let folks know what you expect of *them*.
- ▶ Let folks know how many steps there are in a multistep process.
- ▶ Make sure folks understand the desired outcome of the process they are actually in.
- ▶ Put things where folks expect to find them.
- ▶ Create visible signals that warn of invisible conditions.

Let's take a closer look at these issues.

Knowing what to expect

At the beginning of this chapter, I said that predictability means that something does what you *expect* it to do. Well, *knowing what to expect* is about setting expectations before an interaction actually takes place.

Have you ever bought a guidebook before you went on a vacation to a foreign country or a new city? Probably. I bet you check out comments on Yelp or TripAdvisor before you go to an unfamiliar restaurant. Similarly, you look at the feedback ratings on eBay so you know whether a buyer or seller is trustworthy. Chances are that you also read the reviews on Amazon before you bought this book.

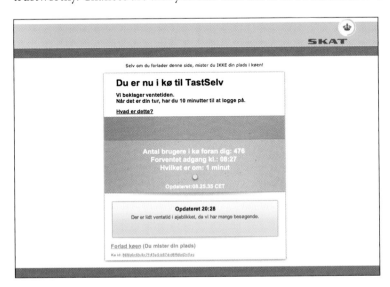

The Danish tax department doesn't have enough servers to handle the online traffic during peak periods. This screen tells taxpayers that there are 476 others in line in front of them and that they can expect to get in at 8:27 AM, which will be in about a minute.

[2] I have some comments on "new and innovative" in the next chapter. It turned out to be something of a rant, so I hope you'll forgive me.

Education	Princeton University
Recommendations	16 people have recommended [illegible]
Connections	500+ connections
Websites	Company Website
	Blog
	RSS feed
Twitter	Follow @[illegible]
Public Profile	http://www.linkedin.com/in/[illegible]

Good education, big personal network, a bunch of recommendations. This individual on LinkedIn exhibits a high degree of trustworthiness.

Branding, customer satisfaction, and expectations

Branding, in the marketing sense, is also about setting expectations. Positioning a product or service in the marketplace is a key part of this. For example, we expect a Volvo to be a safe car. We expect a Jaguar to be a comfortable, yet sporty car. We expect a Chevy to be utilitarian.

Customer satisfaction and expectations go hand-in-hand. For example, some years ago, a survey showed that Walmart, an impersonal discount store with no particular reputation for good service, got better customer satisfaction ratings than Nordstrom, a store that prides itself on service. Why? Because no one really *expects* good service from Walmart, so any little thing the staff does to make your life as a shopper easier seems impressive. For Nordstrom, though, the service bar is set pretty high so it takes a lot more effort to impress their customers. It's the mercantile equivalent of *noblesse oblige*.

So, the lesson here is, if people don't have expectations, help them form these. If they do have expectations, the more you can exceed these expectations, the better the perceived usability. It's never enough just to "meet" expectations in the service world.

"Come back again"? When? In 10 minutes? Tomorrow? Next week? I cannot begin to guess what this shop owner expects me to do.

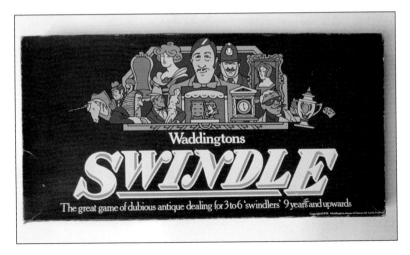

This board game is probably unfamiliar to most people, but the box gives you a pretty good idea what it's about, how many players are involved, and how old kids need to be to enjoy it. This helps a potential purchaser predict whether his or her family will enjoy it. (Cover art copyright 1976, Waddingtons House of Games Ltd.)

Helping set expectations

These days, social media affords a terrific opportunity to communicate and promote your brand, your product, and yourself in an efficient and cost-effective manner. You use discussion forums to start a conversation with your customers (remember, we *all* have customers, even if we are just promoting our ideas). The better you are at creating a dialog using social media, the better you can form the expectations of those who might choose to interact with you at some future time.

Of course, there are also pitfalls. Over the past few years, I've put together a list of 10 social media mistakes, which I'd like to share here, even though these are slightly off-subject:

1. Lying (creating and promoting fake content)
2. Ignoring (thus encouraging negative conversations somewhere else)
3. Denying (openly refusing to acknowledge a problem)
4. Arguing (failure to respect different points of view)
5. Hyping (blatant promotion, inappropriate tone of voice)
6. Gaming (padding ratings)
7. Hiding (no clear points of contact)
8. Hating (actively engaging in a negative manner)
9. Censoring (removing negative comments)
10. Failing to embrace social media

The tone you adopt in social media is critical. Although it may not be as formal as that used for more "official" communications, it still must accurately represent you and your organization. Point

Five is therefore particularly important as this is how good intentions often go terribly wrong. For example, remember the bank I talked about in Chapter Four? Well, here's a recent tweet: "hello tweepers! Are u ready for an awesome friday?" Somehow this just doesn't inspire confidence in a major financial institution.

If you can avoid these mistakes, you'll probably do a much better job creating meaningful, trustworthy expectations.

Instructions revisited—but *never* visited

One of the least effective ways to set expectations is through instructions. People just don't like reading instructions, so don't hide a key piece of information in a "Read Me" text that accompanies your software or bury it in a mammoth printed manual. For example, if people are expecting plug-and-play performance from your product, you'd better make sure it really is plug-and-play. Let me tell you a story.

I bought a new camera recently and a 32 GB memory card. With my previous camera, I just stuck the memory card in the slot on my new laptop and could easily transfer photos; the card performed just like a USB stick and showed up as a "drive" on my desktop. But for some reason, the new card simply wouldn't register with the laptop.

I tried everything I could think of. I Googled the problem like crazy. Finally, someone on a product forum suggested that the driver for the card might be out of date. Although this wasn't actually the solution, it did put me on the right track. It turned out that the driver for the card *reader* was out of date. The fix was relatively easy when I finally figured this out.

But here's the usability problem in terms of predictability: My laptop is only a couple of months old. My *expectation* is that it came with up-to-date drivers as it was able to read all my other memory cards. Moreover, it seems the "new" memory card I bought was actually manufactured *earlier* than my laptop. Therefore, the idea that the laptop itself was at fault never even crossed my mind. And to return to our discussion from Chapter Five about foolproofing, why didn't the laptop at least tell me that it didn't recognize the card and make a suggestion that I check the relevant drivers?

All in all, solving this problem cost me an hour I would gladly have used pursuing something a little less frustrating. On an interesting side note (and because I'm writing a usability book), I spent more than three hours digging through the documentation that came with the laptop looking for some message that I should update the internal drivers. I finally found a relevant instruction on an obscure support CD—one of those many CDs that come with a new computer that usually get thrown out.

Telling folks what *you* expect

Let's assume people have various expectations related to you, your products, and your services. The chances are, you have some expectations of your own. For example, it's probably fair to assume that someone purchasing a sophisticated network-security software package has some idea how computers and networks function. On the other hand, people who buy a basic anti-virus software package might have little idea how it works—or even why it's important ("Well, my son told me to get this. . . .").

The lesson here is that if people need to know something ahead of time, make sure to communicate the information. Consider addressing the follow parameters:

- ▶ Is there specific knowledge people need to have?
- ▶ Are there physical or technical constraints of some kind?
- ▶ Are there geographical constraints of some kind?
- ▶ Is there an age limit?
- ▶ Is there a prequalification process that must be completed first?
- ▶ Is there a time limit?
- ▶ Is there specific information people need to have ready?

The better you communicate these needs up front, the less frustration people will experience. Here are some quick examples of how these parameters play out in real life:

- ▶ "Basic proficiency in written Spanish required."
- ▶ "For Microsoft Windows XP and later."
- ▶ "Cannot be shipped outside the United States."
- ▶ "Purchaser must be 21 years of age or older."
- ▶ "Available by prescription only. Please see your doctor first."
- ▶ "Offer valid thru May 30, 2014."
- ▶ "Please have your account information ready when you call."

Let folks know how many steps are involved

In Chapter Four, I mentioned the "three clicks and you're dead" rule-of-thumb that no longer really holds true (people will click lots of times, as long as they think each click is bringing them closer to their goal). Therefore, it shouldn't come as any surprise that the processes we are able to make the *most* predictable are often those where we tell folks ahead of time how many clicks they will be expected to make.

Shopping carts are a great example of this. The good ones let you know how many steps are involved. The bad ones keep sending you to new forms you have to complete. Airlines, too, are pretty good at explaining how many steps there will be and showing passengers where they are in the booking process.

There really isn't that much more to say except this: If you have a multistep process of some kind, make sure to communicate it in words and/or pictures.

Virtually every airline site has a clearly marked, highly linear reservation process. Here are samples from five major airlines. They are remarkably similar, in terms of both the number of steps and the order of these steps. This helps create predictability, but doesn't necessarily stifle creativity.

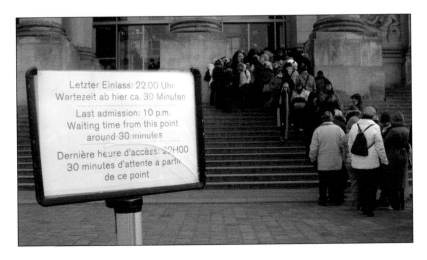

At the Reichstag building in Berlin, visitors are let in in batches of about 30 people. This sign eliminates the frustration of standing in a line that only moves every 15 minutes or so.

Let people know which process they are actually in

We've all waited in long lines only to discover that we are actually in the wrong line. Well, there are lots of processes just like this—both offline and online. Usability problems invariably occur when people think they are doing one thing, but the "stuff" is actually getting them to do something very different. When people have a better understanding of what process they're in, they're also able to predict the type of information they will be asked to provide and the types of things they will be expected to do.

A great example of predictability-gone-wrong is the Wine.com site, which won't even let you look around unless you've chosen a U.S. shipping state. For first-time visitors, this is an unusual and rather unfriendly way to start their customer journey. Visitors don't know why this information is important or even why the question comes up at this particular juncture. Many people undoubtedly think they might be committing themselves to a purchase. In truth, Wine.com is just checking if there are shipping restrictions to the visitor's area, which is reasonable enough even though the approach to the question is confusing.

The proof that this is a clumsy way to handle things is evidenced by the Most Common Questions page under Help—assuming you can spot the tiny Help or Customer Care links on the busy home page. It seems "Where does Wine.com ship wine?" is a question that has been viewed almost 400,000 times! That's about four times as often as any other question on the list. Certainly this suggests that the initial layover screen is not communicating as it should. In fact, if you look at the top 10 questions on the list, almost all of them suggest serious usability problems that relate to a paucity of shared references.

Naturally, if you have a Frequently Asked Questions page (FAQ) or something similar, take a moment to find out *why* some of these questions are on the list. And ask to look at your server logs to see how often people really are looking at them. Perhaps there is a shared-reference issue that can be easily fixed. Or perhaps you don't need an FAQ at all.

The warm-and-fuzzy greeting you get when visiting Wine.com for the first time. There is no way around this screen—it must be answered before your visit can continue.

MOST COMMON QUESTIONS	VIEWS
⚠ **01. Shipping States** - Where does Wine.com ship wine?	393922
⚠ **01. WINE.COM PHONE NUMBER** - How do I call your CUSTOMER CARE department?	119009
⚠ **03. Shipping Rates** - What do you charge for shipping?	38068
⚠ **01. Changing** - How can I make a change to an order already placed?	32176
⚠ **01. Tracking** - How can I check on an order status and delivery?	19001
⚠ **09. Wine Club Member** - How do I cancel an ongoing, month-to-month subscription?	17958
⚠ **04. WEATHER HOLDS** - Why is my order on hold?	13703
⚠ **05. Promotion Codes** - How do I redeem a promotion code?	13398
⚠ **04. Wine Club** - When are wine club orders shipped each month?	11007
⚠ **04. Multiple Charges** - Why is my online statement showing more than one charge?	8153

< View All Common Questions >

Apparently, the opening layover screen at Wine.com doesn't really do the trick, so about 400,000 people have clicked into this FAQ to ask about shipping states. And the other questions suggest a lot of other usability problems, too.

Put things where folks expect to find them

Keeping things visible means putting them where they will be seen. In terms of predictability, it's important also to put things where people expect to find them. For example, in the physical world, I expect light switches to be next to doors. I expect to find pots and pans in the kitchen. I expect the salt to be somewhere near the pepper on the table. In short, I expect to see things fairly close to where I need to use them and grouped in a sensible manner. If I stop by to visit you sometime, I'll probably find your knives and forks in the top drawer in your kitchen.

Basically, this is all about creating designs that encourage retroductive inference—recognizing a pattern from a past experience that can be applied to a new, but related, experience. For this reason, much of the web-related usability research that has taken place over the past 20 years—and the related best-practices—are reflected in the design-pattern libraries now available online. One of the best of these is the Yahoo! Design Pattern Library, originally created and curated by Erin Malone and Christian Crumlish.

Because these design patterns are constantly changing, I don't want to spend a lot of time discussing the individual bits and pieces. I merely urge you to take a look at how others have solved a problem before going off in a completely new direction. And by all means, *do* go off in a new direction if you think that's appropriate. Design libraries shouldn't constrain designers; the libraries should inspire the designers to do even better work. Ultimately, the more people that adopt and adapt these kinds of standardized elements, the easier it will become for people to predict onscreen placement and element behavior even when visiting sites they have never seen before.

Apparently, lots of us usability types study salt shakers—there is less conformity than one might think. Here, the letters send out a clear signal to diners, assuming they speak English.

Here are 10 packets of salt and pepper from various airlines. All packets are oriented with the pepper in the lower portion. Can you see how little consistency or predictability there is in an object often used under poor lighting conditions?

Warn of invisible conditions

Labels, colors, placement, and features can be used to help improve the "scent" of an object so people understand it and can predict its function and behavior. For the most part, when designers talk about "scent," they use it to describe interactive stuff on a screen. But there are lots of good ways to ward off potential problems and guide people offline, too.

Back in school in the chemistry lab, I learned an important rule: Hot glass looks just like cold glass. I still have the scars from an incredibly stupid accident when I was 16. But maybe that's why I tend to notice when stuff is designed in such a way that it signals danger or helps me predict what will happen when I use something.

If you can, consider changes in a physical design so that it sends out a strong nonverbal signal that something is:

▶ Dangerous to touch or approach

▶ Very hot

▶ Very cold

▶ Very sharp

▶ Very bright

▶ Very loud

Obviously, this isn't always possible, but it's worth investigating the options anyway.

The little paper pot-holder on the handle of this silver teapot at the Adlon Hotel in Berlin sends a clear signal that the handle is hot. And it turns a potential problem into a memorable service-design experience.

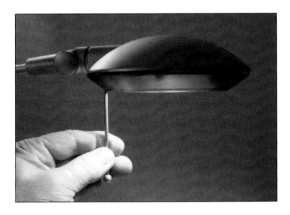

This desk lamp has a special handle so you don't get burned when you adjust the shade. Not only does the handle send out a signal that this is the place to hold, it also helps prevent the hot bulb from getting too near things that could burn.

Although some international symbols are fairly widely recognized, I hadn't seen this one until I noticed it on an electrical junction box in Spain. Because the box was on the side of a church, the sign took on a whole new meaning—and I took a picture.

▶ A SHORT INTRODUCTION TO MCDONALDIZATION
A TALE FROM THE TRENCHES

QUICK QUIZ. WHAT COMES NEXT?

▶ Big Mac®

▶ Shake

▶ ???

Even folks who have never even seen a McDonald's often know the answer.[4] Personally, I love McDonald's because I don't have to think. I know how the lines and ordering process work. I know how much food to order to suit my appetite. I know how much it will cost. I know how long it will take to prepare. I know how long it will take to eat. It is about as predictable an experience as one can have in life.

Yet recently, in two different franchises, I was horrified to learn they didn't serve Quarter Pounders with Cheese, which has been my standard burger for more than 40 years.

"Would you like to try our Caesar Salad with Grilled Chicken or our new Big 'N Tasty® burger?" asked the well-trained girl behind the counter. Er . . . well . . . no. I don't really come to McDonald's for culinary adventure.

"What happened to Quarter Pounders?" I asked with growing trepidation.

"We like to vary our menu so people don't get bored with our food."

Whoa! How many billions of burgers has this company sold? And now they're scared we'll get bored with their burgers? This sudden unpredictability really caught me off guard. It also violated a rather well-known sociological model.

In 1993, a sociologist by the name of George Ritzer came up with a modern alternative to the much earlier theories of rationalization espoused by German sociologist Max Weber. Ritzer claimed that the fast food restaurant had taken the place of bureaucracy in the model of rationalization. Ritzer defined the four components of "McDonaldization" as

▶ **Efficiency:** Employing the best and least wasteful route toward each goal

▶ **Calculability:** Emphasizing quantity over quality

[4]The answer is "fries."

> ### A SHORT INTRODUCTION TO MCDONALDIZATION
> #### A TALE FROM THE TRENCHES
>
> ---
>
> > **Predictability:** Uniformity across settings and times
> > **Control:** Taking skills away from people
>
> Now, for employees, this paints a pretty grim picture. But look at the role of predictability. It's the only one of the four components that actually provides any degree of value to the customer.
>
> So, McDonald's, if you're going to step outside the model that bears your name, I urge you to focus on changing a *different* component. And please, *please* bring back Quarter Pounders in all of your restaurants.

TEN WAYS TO HELP PEOPLE PREDICT THE FUTURE

1. Are you helping people draw on past experiences? If not, can you create the cognitive trigger?

2. Are there things people should know ahead of time? Can you find ways to let them know in a logical, unobtrusive way?

3. Have you let people know what you expect of them? Do they need special talents or to meet some prerequisite? If so, is this clearly communicated before they get too deep into a process?

4. Does your stuff feature multistep processes? Is the number of steps announced ahead of time or do you need to fine-tune your communications and/or design?

5. Are people trying to solve one specific task when you are actually trying to get them to solve an entirely different task to meet your own needs? Can you separate the two processes or at least let folks know that they need to do you a favor in order to get stuff to work properly?

6. Have you looked at design patterns that relate to your own designs? Are you following best practices? If not, why not?

7. Can you provide visible signals of some kind that will indicate possible dangers—particularly physical dangers?

8. If you are using social-media tools, are you making any of the 10 mistakes mentioned earlier in this chapter?

9. Are you relying on instructions to make your designs work? Can you eliminate traditional manuals and read-me texts by creating task-relevant messages that appear only when needed?

10. Is anything happening when you use your stuff that takes you slightly by surprise? Are there things that don't entirely function as you expect them to?

OTHER BOOKS
YOU MIGHT LIKE

We predict the future by examining the past. Here are a couple of books that can get your cognitive juices flowing.

▶ *Designing Social Interfaces*, Christian Crumlish and Erin Malone, O'Reilly, 2009

▶ *Search Patterns*, Peter Morville and Jeffery Callender, O'Reilly, 2010

▶ *Social Media ROI: Managing and Measuring Social Media Efforts in Your Organization*, Olivier Blanchard, Que, 2011

▶ *Why Things Bite Back: Technology and the Revenge of Unintended Consequences*, Edward Tenner, Vintage, 1996

THINGS TO
GOOGLE

▶ Design pattern library
▶ Predictability in design
▶ McDonaldization
▶ George Ritzer
▶ Light switches - Mumbai, India

Chapter Eleven

Next steps

Remember Bogo Vatovec's three-step usability plan? I told you about it in the Introduction to this book. Here it is again if you skipped ahead:

▶ Nobody talks about usability.

▶ Everybody talks about usability.

▶ Nobody talks about usability.

I'll assume nobody is talking about usability in your company, but you just read a book and you're feeling inspired. I'm also going to assume that when it comes to improving usability, you're on your own, without help, without money, and with limited time. Here are some sad facts:

▶ All "stuff" has usability problems.

▶ There are never enough resources to fix the problems.

Accept this and move on. Don't dwell on *why* something is lousy, but figure out how to make it *better*. You *can* do a lot of things on your own— and if you can get your design team motivated, all the better. If you can get the big bosses to understand that "there's gold in them thar tests . . ." that's gold indeed![1]

[1] Dahlonega, Georgia was where the first U.S. gold rush took place in 1828. Dahlonega Mint assayer Dr. M. F. Stephenson is famously misquoted as having said, "There's gold in them thar hills," to miners headed for California in 1849. He was referring to his own hills, of course, in an attempt to keep the local mines open and himself employed.

Guerilla-style usability

Now that you've read this book, here's how to put it to practical use.

First, with your particular "stuff" in mind, take another look at the 10 lists that conclude each chapter. From each of these, choose *one* item that you think you can work on, without either a lot of assistance or a lot of money.

Armed with your basic list of 10 issues (one task from each chapter), make notes as to what you would improve and how you would accomplish it. Don't worry about *why* something is as it is, but think about how it *could be*. Along the way, ask friends, colleagues, and family for their opinions about any aspects that are puzzling you. Some of their answers and suggestions will be idiotic, but I assure you some will also be useful.

Now, refine your notes and make a list of 10 very specific things that you want to change. Then, prioritize this list twice, in two different ways:

▶ Mission-critical changes (things that can make or break a conversion)

▶ Small wins, easy fixes (things that don't take a lot of time or effort to correct and provide incremental improvements)

If anything from your original list landed near the top of both of your prioritized lists, do this task *first*; it's both easy and important. But don't forget the other stuff. Make a schedule and set things in motion.

Finally, set a deadline for yourself (or your team) that enables you to realistically complete the changes you've identified. And when you're done, it's time to start again with a new list of 10 things.

Formalized think-aloud tests

Although you might not choose to do actual usability tests, here's how it's done.

The preferred method of usability testing, at least for online applications, is the "think-aloud" test. Here, a test subject is asked to complete various tasks, such as filling out a form, finding a piece of information, or making a judgment based on several pieces of information. These tasks make up what is known as the "test protocol."

The test subject is ideally part of the target group for the application and from outside the organization. Friends and family can sometimes fill in if it's not possible to get a true outsider. Be careful though, about recruiting folks from within the company as they tend not to be as critical as they should be. You need to find people who are honest, not diplomatic.

The test subject is asked to think aloud while working on the tasks. For example:

"Hmm. I don't know what to do. I think clicking on the big red button might be a good idea. (click) Whoa. How did I get here? Oh, wait, here's the link I want. (click) Why do I have to click twice to get to this page? I'm having trouble finding the information I want, but I'm pretty sure it must be here somewhere. . . ."

During this test, a facilitator/observer sits next to the test subject and watches what's going on and takes notes. If the test subject goes silent, the facilitator urges them on with questions such as:

▶ "What are you thinking now?"

▶ "What are you looking at?"

▶ "What do you want to do now?"

You can learn a lot from these tests. And if you get your designers to sit in and observe (if they can keep their mouths shut), it's often a shock for them to see how people struggle with their designs. Don't worry about offending anyone on your team; because these tests represent truly impartial, constructive criticism, they are rarely taken the wrong way.

What I've described here is very bare bones. Professional facilitators will have lots of legitimate complaints regarding my advice. But if you have no budget and little support within your organization, this is a workable way to get things going. In fact, even if you only conduct tests like these for one hour each month, you'll be surprised at how valuable they can be.

Making usability part of the business case

You want people to buy your product. Or use your service. Or agree with your ideas. Ultimately, the success of your product, service, or idea hinges on how the market reacts to your offering. Good usability, like sunshine, makes good things even more appealing. And the better your stuff works, the more of your goals will be met—whatever these may be.

Your task when convincing colleagues who seriously out-rank you is to show the potential gains that can be achieved through usability. To do this, you need to establish a baseline. After all, you can't demonstrate improvement if you don't know where things were before you started.

If you're working strictly online, make sure you have solid data from an analytics program, such as Google Analytics. That said, sophisticated content-management systems also include online marketing suites and "customer engagement platforms" that are very sexy indeed. But if you already have one of these installed with your content management system (CMS), then your organization is probably paying attention to usability already. For now, I'm assuming that you're still a "rogue usability advocate."

Use these data to demonstrate where things go right and where things go wrong. Then show how minor changes in functionality, design, and content can improve the conversions. For example, if a page on a website has a "bounce rate" of 89 percent, that's something that needs investigating.[2] If this is just a basic informational page and the average time on the page is two minutes, then the page is probably working. But if the page is part of a conversion funnel and people are clicking the back button after a few seconds, even though other link options were available, you have a problem.[3] So, armed with the bounce-rate information and some ideas as to why things aren't working, make a projection that demonstrates the potential monetary gains that can be achieved by carrying out the changes you suggest.

Baby steps, I agree. But this is a start. And it is do-able, even when the powers that be won't support you wholeheartedly.

If you are dealing with physical stuff, you'll undoubtedly find that changing a manufacturing process is going to be difficult. The degree to which you can get your ideas adopted will depend on four things:

▶ Your clout within the organization

▶ The degree of difficulty in changing the manufacturing process

▶ The degree to which the changes you suggest may affect existing warranties on products that have already been shipped

▶ Your ability to show how your usability improvements will reduce costs or improve sales

Sometimes, small changes in a sticker on a product can produce fantastic results. Or simple text changes in the documentation or packaging. So don't give up—there is always low-hanging usability fruit somewhere.

If you're dealing with services, your task will be to show those who are providing the service that by adopting your suggestions they will:

▶ Deal with fewer customer complaints

▶ Enjoy an easier, less stressful job

▶ Receive more respect from colleagues and customers alike

▶ Cut costs

And this isn't spin. This is really what happens when service providers get their acts together. You *can* get your front line to care about your bottom line!

YOU HAVE NOW COMPLETED THE OFFICIAL PART OF THIS BOOK. WHAT FOLLOWS ARE THREE STORIES YOU MIGHT FIND USEFUL IN YOUR QUEST TO BUILD A BETTER WORLD.

---

[2] A bounce rate is when people click to a page, but quickly leave again without further interaction.

[3] A conversion funnel is part of the path that leads potential customers from a basic informational web page to an onscreen form through which they give you money and/or personal details.

Invention or innovation?

Webster's Dictionary defines innovation as "the introduction of something new; a new idea, method, or device." But this definition is misleading. Although innovation *is* usually something new, just because it *is* new doesn't necessarily make it innovative.

I firmly believe there is only one reason to innovate and that is to *solve a problem*. And if you don't solve a problem, you are going to create one. In other words, innovation is always a *planned process*.

This also means that invention (which often occurs accidentally) is actually a step prior to innovation. Let me give you an example:

Throughout the 1890s, Gugliemo Marconi experimented with radio-telegraphy. In December 1894, he sent the first wireless transmission. And in 1909, he shared the Nobel Prize in Physics with Karl Braun for his contributions to the development of wireless telegraphy.[4] But is this also innovation?

No. The real innovation came on April 15, 1912 when 710 passengers and crew from the ill-fated steamer *R.M.S. Titanic* were rescued in the mid-Atlantic, thanks to the wireless distress signal received by other ships in the area. Marconi's invention solved a problem. The *planned process* was to adopt wireless telegraphy to help ships communicate when they were too far away from shore or other ships to use flags, skyrockets, horns, and other signals.

But the story of the *Titanic* doesn't end here; a nearby ship, the *Californian*, did not respond to the SOS because their radio operator had already gone to bed. The result was new legislation that required ships to man their wireless stations 24/7. A best-practice was born.

In short, invention leads to innovation, which in turn leads to best practice. The next round of innovation builds on current best practices. And the cycle continues forever.

Some innovations are incremental, such as the Roman courier system, *cursus publicus*, which led to formalized mail systems, which were eventually supplemented by the fax. In each instance, getting a message from one place to another became faster and more efficient. But other innovations are disruptive. For example, e-mail is not just an easier way to send documents; e-mail (and the related attachments) enables us to work on the *same* document as our colleagues on the other side of the world.

Not surprisingly, most companies adopted the fax fairly rapidly. Yet it took years before companies felt comfortable sending editable documents to others. In legal terms, there is still discussion as to what constitutes an "original" document these days.

Finally, each time you innovate (that is to say solve a problem), your actions will have technological, social, and political consequences. Would-be innovators need to be aware of this: Innovative solutions can often have unexpected consequences if all three issues are not taken into account.

[4]There is now much evidence to suggest that Nicola Tesla should have been awarded the prize instead of Marconi, but that's a different story.

Your task is to make sure your design team understands the difference between invention and innovation. Don't let them do "new" stuff just for the sake of being different. Solve a problem!

In 1894, Gugliemo Marconi sent the first wireless transmission. And in 1909, he shared the Nobel Prize in Physics with Karl Braun for his contributions to the development of wireless telegraphy.

Accidents can never be attributed to a single cause

If you ask people why the *Titanic* sank, most will say, "It hit an iceberg." Which is true. But *why* did it hit an iceberg? And *why* did this cause it to sink?

In almost every disaster, there is never just a single *why*. If we examine the story of the *Titanic*, here are some of the many contributing factors:

▶ The ship was travelling fairly fast at 22 knots.

▶ The iceberg was further south than icebergs usually were at that time of year.

▶ A critical ice warning was not relayed from the radio operator to the captain.

▶ The sea was dead calm so the iceberg showed no wake. That meant it was spotted too late for the ship to turn sufficiently.

▶ Some marine architects suggest the rudder may have been too small to quickly turn a ship of this size.

▶ The rivets that held the ship together were of substandard quality and became particularly brittle in cold water.

▶ The watertight bulkheads didn't go up high enough, permitting water to spill over from one compartment to the next as the ship sank.

▶ If the *Titanic* had not seen the iceberg at all, but just plowed into it head on, the ship might have survived.

If any one of these factors had been a little different, a catastrophe might have been avoided. But, hey, that's the way these things work.

So, take another look at that list of 10 things I asked you to prepare. You might find that a single quick-fix or easy change can produce miraculous results.

Don't draw a conclusion based on an isolated incident

The *Titanic* is a textbook example of why excessive generalization from a single observation is a statistically poor model. In the case of the *Titanic*, which took more than two and a half hours to sink, on a fairly even keel, in a calm sea, the passengers could have been saved if there had been enough lifeboats. The conclusion was that ships should have lifeboat capacity for everyone on board.

Yet neither before nor since the *Titanic* has a ship sunk in such a fortuitous manner.[5] Most ships sink quickly. They often develop heavy lists, making it impossible to launch boats. Extra boats can clutter up deck space, making it harder to launch those boats that *can* be launched. Finally, the extra weight of the lifeboats can make some ships top-heavy and therefore more dangerous.

And these are some of the reasons the *Titanic* had fewer seats in lifeboats than passengers—as did most ships of her era. However, a few years later, the *S.S. Eastland* did have "boats for all"—a direct result of the LaFollett Seaman's Act, signed into law by U.S. President Wilson on March 4, 1915. And that brings me to the last of my three stories.

On July 2, 1915, the *S.S. Eastland*, a Great Lakes excursion steamer out of Chicago, received additional lifeboats to reflect her licensed capacity of 2,500 passengers. And on July 24, 1915, the first time she was fully loaded, the dangerously top-heavy ship capsized right at her dock. More than 800 Western Electric employees headed for a company picnic drowned. Not a single lifeboat could be launched.

So, beware of so-called "best practices" that are based on little or no statistical evidence. That also means be careful not to jump to conclusions when interpreting isolated statistics from customer-satisfaction surveys and web-analytics applications, or when listening to the opinions of a single, but vocal, member of your team.

[5]Here are some time-to-sink statistics from other major ship disasters: *Empress of Ireland* (1914), 14 minutes; *Lusitania* (1915), 18 minutes; *Eastland* (1915), two minutes; *Britannic* (1916), 55 minutes (1916); *Andrea Doria* (1956), 11 hours (but due to a heavy list only half of her boats could be launched); *Herald of Free Enterprise* (1987), 90 seconds; *Doña Paz* (1987), two hours (but was engulfed in fire); *Estonia* (1994), 55 minutes (in a violent storm); *Le Joola* (2002), under five minutes.

One of the *Titanic's* Engelhardt collapsible lifeboats. In all,
710 people were saved thanks to another ship, the *Carpathia*,
which heroically responded to the world's first SOS signal on the
night of April 15, 1912.

The first time the *S.S. Eastland* was loaded to capacity, she turned
turtle next to her dock on the Chicago River. More than 800 people
drowned. It turns out that the weight of her extra lifeboats was a
contributing factor in the disaster.

OTHER BOOKS YOU MIGHT LIKE

Alright. I admit this is a hodge-podge of stuff. But it's all relevant (in strangely bizarre ways).

- ▶ *Actionable Web Analytics: Using Data to Make Smart Business Decisions*, Jason Burby and Shane Atchison, Wiley, 2007

- ▶ *Eastland: Legacy of the Titanic*, George W. Hilton, Stanford University Press, 1995

- ▶ *Getting Them to Give a Damn: How to Get Your Front Line to Care about Your Bottom Line*, Eric Chester, Dearborn, 2005

- ▶ *Handbook of Usability Testing: How to Plan, Design, and Conduct Effective Tests*, Jeffrey Rubin and Dana Chisnell, Wiley, 2008

- ▶ *The Innovator's Dilemma: When New Technologies Cause Great Firms to Fail*, Clayton M. Christensen, Harvard Business School Press, 1997

- ▶ *The Innovator's Solution: Creating and Sustaining Successful Growth*, Clayton M. Christensen and Michael E. Raynor, Harvard Business School Press, 2003

- ▶ *The Last Log of the Titanic: What Really Happened on the Doomed Ship's Bridge?*, David G. Brown, McGraw Hill, 2001

- ▶ *Measuring the User Experience: Collecting, Analyzing, and Presenting Usability Metrics*, Tom Tullis and Bill Albert, Morgan Kaufmann, 2008

- ▶ *Rocket Surgery Made Easy: The Do-It-Yourself Guide to Finding and Fixing Usability Problems*, Steve Krug, New Riders, 2010

THINGS TO GOOGLE

▶ Think-aloud test

▶ Usability test protocols

▶ Usability test facilitation

▶ Guerilla usability

▶ Web analytics

▶ Online business models

▶ Service design ROI

▶ Innovation

▶ Clayton Christensen

▶ Disaster scenarios

▶ *RMS Titanic*

▶ *Eastland* disaster

BIBLIOGRAPHY

Each of the chapters in this book ends with a suggested-reading list. At the risk of some repetition, here are the books I feel make up a good basic library for anyone seriously interested in product design, service design, website design, user-experience design, and related fields.

Analytics

Measuring the User Experience: Collecting, Analyzing, and Presenting Usability Metrics, Tom Tullis and Bill Albert, Morgan Kaufmann, 2008

Search Analytics for Your Site: Conversations with Your Customers, Louis Rosenfeld, Rosenfeld, 2011

Social Media Metrics: How to Measure and Optimize Your Marketing Investment, Jim Sterne, Wiley, 2010

Social Media ROI: Managing and Measuring Social Media Efforts in Your Organization, Olivier Blanchard, Que, 2011

Web Analytics an Hour a Day, Avinash Kaushik, Sybex, 2007

Cognition

100 Things Every Designer Needs to Know About People, Susan M. Weinschenk, New Riders, 2011

How We Decide, Jonah Lehrer, Mariner, 2009

Irrationality, Stuart Sutherland, Constable and Co., 1992

A Mind of Its Own: How Your Brain Distorts and Deceives, Cordelia Fine, Icon, 2005

Neuro Web Design: What Makes Them Click, Susan M. Weinschenk, New Riders, 2009

Persuasive Technology: Using Computers to Change What We Think and Do, B.J. Fogg, Morgan Kaufmann, 2003

Predictably Irrational: The Hidden Forces That Shape Our Decisions, Dan Ariely, HarperCollins, 2009

Content creation

Clout: The Art and Science of Influential Web Content, Colleen Jones, New Riders, 2011

Killer Web Content: Make the Sale, Deliver the Service, Build the Brand, Gerry McGovern, A&C Black, 2006

Letting Go of the Words: Writing Web Content That Works, Ginny Redish, Morgan Kaufmann, 2007

Content strategy

Content Strategy at Work: Real-World Stories to Strengthen Every Interactive Project, Margot Bloomstein, Morgan Kaufmann, 2012

Content Strategy for the Web, Kristina Halvorson and Melissa Rach, New Riders 2012

The Web Content Strategist's Bible: The Complete Guide to a New and Lucrative Career For Writers Of All Kinds, Richard Sheffield, CreateSpace, 2009

Design research

Contextual Design: Defining Customer-Centered Systems, Hugh Beyer and Karen Holtzblatt, Morgan Kaufmann, 1998

Observing the User Experience: A Practitioner's Guide to User Research, Mike Kuniavsky, Morgan Kaufmann, 2003

Industrial design

The Design of Everyday Things, Donald A. Norman, Basic Books, 2002

Designing for People, Henry Dreyfuss, Simon and Schuster, 1955

Handbook of Human Factors and Ergonomics, Gavriel Salvendy, Wiley, 2006

Living with Complexity, Donald A. Norman, MIT Press, 2011

Information architecture

Information Architecture: Blueprints for the Web, Christina Wodtke and Austin Govella, New Riders, 2009

Information Architecture for the World Wide Web, Peter Morville and Louis Rosenfeld, O'Reilly, 2006

Pervasive Information Architecture: Designing Cross-Channel User Experiences, Andrea Resmini and Luca Rosati, Morgan Kaufmann, 2011

Interactive design (general)

Designing for the Digital Age: How to Create Human-Centered Products and Services, Kim Goodwin, Wiley, 2009

Designing Interactions, Bill Moggridge, MIT Press, 2007

Designing the User Interface: Strategies for Effective Human-Computer Interaction, Ben Shneiderman and Catherine Plaisant, Addison Wesley, 2005

The Elements of User Experience: User-Centered Design for the Web, Jesse James Garrett, New Riders, 2003

Interactive design (specific subjects)

Brave NUI World: Designing Natural User Interfaces for Touch and Gesture, Daniel Wigdor and Dennis Wixon, Morgan Kaufmann, 2011

Defensive Design for the Web: How to Improve Error Messages, Help, Forms, and Other Crisis Points, Matthew Linderman with Jason Fried (37 signals), New Riders, 2004

Designing Gestural Interfaces: Touchscreens and Interactive Devices, Dan Saffer, O'Reilly, 2008

Designing Interfaces, Jenifer Tidwell, O'Reilly, 2005

Designing Search: UX Strategies for eCommerce Success, Greg Nudelman, Wiley, 2011

Designing for the Social Web, Joshua Porter, New Riders, 2008

Designing Social Interfaces: Principles, Patterns, and Practices for Improving the User Experience, Christian Crumlish and Erin Malone, O'Reilly, 2009

Designing Web Navigation: Optimizing the User Experience, James Kalbach, O'Reilly, 2007

Designing Web Interfaces: Principles and Patterns for Rich Interactions, Bill Scott and Theresa Neil, O'Reilly, 2009

Forms that Work: Designing Web Forms for Usability, Caroline Jarrett and Gerry Gaffney, Morgan Kaufmann, 2009

Sketching User Experiences: Getting the Design Right and the Right Design, Bill Buxton, Morgan Kaufmann, 2007

The User Is Always Right: A Practical Guide to Creating and Using Personas for the Web, Steve Mulder with Ziv Yaar, New Riders, 2006

Web Anatomy: Interaction Design Frameworks that Work, Robert Hoekman, Jr. and Jared Spool, New Riders, 2010

Web Forms Design: Filling in the Blanks, Luke Wroblewski, Rosenfeld Media, 2008

What Every Intranet Team Should Know, James Robertson, Step Two Designs, 2009

Project management

A Project Guide to UX Design: For User Experience Designers in the Field or in the Making, Second Edition, Russ Unger and Carolyn Chandler, New Riders, 2012

User Experience Management: Essential Skills for Leading Effective UX Teams, Arnie Lund, Morgan Kaufmann, 2011

Prototyping and documentation

Communicating Design: Developing Web Site Documentation for Design and Planning, Dan Brown, New Riders, 2012

Paper Prototyping: The Fast and Easy Way to Design and Refine User Interfaces, Carolyn Snyder, Morgan Kaufmann, 2003

Prototyping: A Practitioner's Guide, Todd Zaki Warfel, Rosenfeld, 2009

Service design

This Is Service Design Thinking: Basics, Tools, Cases, Marc Stickdorn and Jakob Schneider, BIS, 2011

WAYMISH: Why Are You Making It So Hard For Me To Give You My Money?, Ray Considine and Ted Cohn, Waymish Publishing, 2000

Usability

Don't Make Me Think: A Common Sense Approach to Web Usability, Second Edition, Steve Krug, New Riders, 2006

Handbook of Usability Testing: How to Plan, Design, and Conduct Effective Tests, Jeffrey Rubin and Dana Chisnell, Wiley, 2008

Simple and Usable Web, Mobile, and Interaction Design, Giles Colborne, New Riders, 2011

Prioritizing Web Usability, Jakob Nielsen and Hoa Loranger, New Riders, 2006

INDEX

logic and, 159
navigation, 5, 14
restaurants, 16, 142, 165
retroductive inference, 158, 175–176, 189
Robinson, Hilary, 16
Rocket Surgery Made Easy: The Do-It-Yourself Guide to Finding and Fixing Usability Problems (Krug), 215
Roddick, Ellen, 155
Rolls-Royce purchase, 39–40
rope and wood, parked airplane, 4
Rosenfeld, Louis, 108
round spoon, square bowl, 4
routines
  repeatable, 100–101
  switching, 67–69
Royal Air Force blind-flying controls, 179
Royal Bank of Scotland, silent usher, 59
Rubin, Jeffrey, 215
Russian Federation form, 10

sales taxes, currency and, 151
Salvendy, Gavriel, 62
Samsung site error, 139
Samsung Ultra Touch, 124
SAS boarding pass, barcode, 44
sauna, eyeglass holder, 66
scaling up, cutting down, 28, 41
Scandic Hotel buffet, 161
Scandinavian Airlines, in-flight map, 148
scent, cognitive clues, 31, 123, 146, 200
Scott, Bill, 42
scrolling
  "fold" concept, 115–122
  myth, 144
  scroll-friendly pages, 123
  statistics, 116, 144
Search Analytics for Your Site (Rosenfeld), 108
search for things. *See* Google
Search Patterns (Morville & Callender), 205
Sears, Roebuck & Co shoe page, 145
Sears vacuum-cleaner bags, 79–81

sensory feedback. *See* feedback
setting expectations, 193–194
shared references, 137–155. *See also* understandability
  alarm button, 161
  books, 155
  creating, keys, 141–143
  defined, 138
  "light bulb" test, 139–140
  predictability, 189
  understandability, 137–138
Sharratt, Nick, 16
Sheraton Four Points hotel, 113
Sheremetyevo Airport, 179
ship disasters, 212–214, 215, 216
shoe page, 145
silent usher, 58–59, 62
Simple and Usable (Colborne), 188
simple instructions, 96–98
sink stopper design, 190
Sistine Chapel, smoke, 190
Skype issues, 70, 121
smart TVs, 7, 27, 41, 48
smartphones
  clocks, 71
  company, con artists, 153
  driving directions, 71
  QR codes, 99
  scrolling, 124
SmartPlanet, 70
smoke, Sistine Chapel, 190
Social Media ROI: Managing and Measuring Social Media Efforts in Your Organization (Blanchard), 205
someone might want this, 73
Souders, Steve, 14
sounds, shared reference, 138
sounds, task completion, 36
spa bath controls, 160
speed, processing, 5, 14–15
speed bumps, 102
speed-limit signs, Danish, 184–186
spelling errors, 32, 95–96
square bowl, round spoon, 4
standardization, consistency and, 177–178
Stanton, Neville A., 108
State, required field, 9–10, 20
state change, 26
state the obvious, 100
static load, fatigue and, 46

stereotypes, archetypes, 73
stretch, move, exercise, 46
Studio 7.5, 136
Stumblehere.com, 127
subdomain wildcard, 95
Sunstein, Cass R., 170
Sutherland, Stuart, 170
Swindle board game, 193
switching from online to offline, 70–71
switching interfaces, 69–70
switching routines, 67–69
synonyms, consistency, 172

tabbing, mouse movements and, 53–54
Tales from the Trenches
  blooming flower problem, 49, 60–61
  Cadillac navigation system, 167–168
  Danish speed-limit signs, 184–186
  exploding chicken alfredo, 104–106
  McDonaldization, 202–203
  mobile phone company, con artists, 153
  NAACP donation, 19–22, 98
  perks of business travel, 132–134
  Rolls-Royce purchase, 39–40
  vacuum-cleaner bags, 79–81
task completion, design patterns, 36
Tastebook.com, iPad and, 55
taxes, currency and, 151
Tenner, Edward, 205
Terms and Conditions, 96, 97, 114
Tesla, Nicola, 211
Thaler, Richard H., 170
thermostat inconsistency, 180
Things to Google. *See* Google
think-aloud tests, 208–209
three clicks and you're dead, 77–78, 195–196
timing issues, nested navigation menus, 49–50
Titanic ship, 211, 212–213, 214, 215
title, metadata, 96
Tognazzini, Bruce, 172
toilet stall, burned wall, 72
touch-screen devices, mouseploration, 33